LOST & FOUND

Lost & Found

ELLEN UZELAC

WRS
PUBLISHING

A Division of WRS Group, Inc.
Waco, Texas

To share responses to "Lost & Found: A Journey Through Grief," you may write: Ellen Uzelac c/o 30043 Grandpoint Lane, Rancho Palos Verdes, CA 90274.

First published in the United States of America in 1994 by WRS Publishing, A Division of WRS Group, Inc., 701 N. New Road, Waco, Texas 76710
Book design by Kenneth Turbeville
Jacket design by Linda Filgo

10 9 8 7 6 5 4 3 2 1

Library of Congress Catalog Card Number

ISBN 1-56796-043-x

DEDICATION

For Aimée and Anne

TABLE OF CONTENTS

PREFACE

I began to miss Jim even before he died. One of the most difficult things I've ever done was to sing "Happy Birthday" to him on his 41st birthday, knowing it would be his last.

The cancer had come suddenly, insinuating itself into our lives like an unexpected house guest. It arrived unbidden, a stranger. But before long it was to clutch us in its embrace like the closest of intimates. Slowly and silently it stole Jim's life, and forever changed mine.

Until then, the closest I had ever been to death were the stories I had covered for newspapers—murders, fires, an airplane crash. But those tragedies belonged to other people and, after a brief engagement with them, I was able to walk away.

Death, it seemed, had kept me at a safe distance. As far as I knew, when something was broken, you got it fixed. When something was lost, you replaced it. A hurt wasn't anything that a loving hug and kind words couldn't cure.

It wasn't going to be that way this time. There were only six months between Jim's diagnosis and death, and that long, final moment that ended his life seemed to define my own. That's when I started counting time and measuring life's contents.

On a warm, spring day in 1987, at the age of thirty-one, I woke up married and went to sleep a widow. For months I could not look in a mirror without seeing Jim looking back. I wouldn't leave the house without photographs of him. I kissed them, talked to them, shouted at them. I slept with his worn leather motorcycle jacket over me, hoping to smell something of him in it.

Whenever I did go out, I was certain everyone could guess that my husband had just died. Surely, my face gave it away. My skin was stretched taut over my bones and my voice came out thin and flat—as if it was coming from another spot in the room. I felt amputated and adrift, marooned in unfamiliar landscape.

Jim's death had changed my habitat and set me wandering. Watching night fall over the San Francisco Bay from my living room window not long after he died, I decided to embrace the grieving process. If Jim could no longer be my companion, then grief would be, and for many months it was grief that filled the hole where my heart had been. It became the only nourishment I knew, but I discovered that while it sapped my strength and challenged my understanding, it also gave me back my heart.

What follows is not a manual on how to surmount grief. It is a prescription for hope.

CHAPTER
1

THE DIAGNOSIS

There was nothing unusual about the day my husband started dying. It was just past noon on a Monday and Jim, an editor at *The Baltimore Sun*, was sequestered with his boss in a cramped office so close to my own desk that I could hear the murmur of Jim's voice.

As I waited for Jim to emerge from his meeting, my mind wandered back to our weekend in western Maryland, where we'd gone to celebrate an early Christmas with friends. As soon as we arrived at our friends' house, Jim jumped out of our battered Plymouth, ran to the curb and vomited into the gutter.

"You OK?" I asked as I rubbed his back through the thick skin of his leather jacket. He'd been sick a lot lately. Jim's vomit mixed with the dirty snow and I remember wondering whether it would freeze. Afterward, as we sat on the curb holding hands, the icy temperature caused us both to tremble. I could see our friend, Sue, inside the front door, peering at us with eyes sharpened into question marks. I gave her a half-hearted wave.

Jim had been ill for two weeks with headaches, fatigue and, now, nausea. His doctor had said he was suffering from migraine headaches and not to worry. I didn't— lots of people have migraines. I just couldn't understand why the pills that had been prescribed weren't working.

Jim had spent most of the weekend curled up on a couch next to a freshly cut Christmas tree in the living room, dozing in the thick scent of Scotch pine. His lack of spirit infuriated me. "Slug," I kept calling him. "Slug." I cannot hear that word now without grimacing.

By Monday, Jim was feeling better and, after his meeting, we were planning to go out for chili at a diner down the street. We ate together most days, a welcome change after working different shifts for two years. During his discussion with editor Tom Linthicum, Jim turned off the overhead light, saying the glare hurt his eyes. "It's the headache," Jim explained as the two men conferred in near darkness. "I can't seem to shake it." He had taken sick days most of the previous week, felled by the constant thudding in his head. As they finished talking, Jim rose to his feet, leaned his five-foot-ten frame against a wall and slowly sank into the gray carpet.

There were voices and yelling. "Jim's collapsed! Jim's blacked out!" The voices seemed to be yelling at me. I heard someone call my name, "Ellen!" Then, "Come quickly. He's collapsed." I stood up, looked toward the office and said, "No." My feet were stuck to the floor, frozen in place like an ice statue. An editor, Karol Menzie, finally pushed me into the office where Jim lay, his face hidden in his arms to cover his embarrassment. I knelt on the floor beside him, wondering what I was supposed to do. I wished everyone would go away and leave us alone. We had been thrown into a drama without our permission and the attention we were getting from our flustered colleagues made me feel naked and vulnerable.

"It's OK," Jim announced to the heads hanging over him. "I'm all right." But I didn't believe him. I don't think anyone did. All I could think of was that Jim was sprawled awkwardly across the floor and he was wearing my beige Levi cords, the ones with the hole in the left front pocket. Somehow, the fact that he was wearing my jeans consoled me.

Moments later, an officious company nurse appeared with a wheelchair and insisted she accompany Jim to the emergency room at Mercy Hospital, a two-block walk from the newspaper building. I'm sure he wouldn't have gone without her prodding.

I wheeled Jim out of the newsroom, into an elevator and outside onto Calvert Street, one of Baltimore's main avenues. "It's only a headache," he kept saying. "A headache, that's all." On the way to the hospital, we passed The Bridge, the down-home diner with plucky waitresses and giveaway prices where we had planned to go for lunch. To Jim, a good chow-down was fire-hot chili, bread slathered with butter and a cigarette after, except that he'd stopped smoking a few months earlier. I envied the people inside. Something as simple as lunch suddenly seemed precious.

A few hours later, inside an airless examining room at Mercy Hospital, the doctors told us they had found a brain tumor on the right side of Jim's head. It would change everything we had ever known.

We learned that when a cancer metastasizes, it spreads, and that when pain is palliated, it is lessened. The rhythm of hospitals was to become as familiar to us as the beating of our own hearts. We became ardent students of cancer, believing that if we got to know it well enough we could somehow outsmart it.

As I think back on it, I began losing Jim the instant the automatic glass doors of the emergency room slammed shut behind us. For me, the short walk down Calvert Street on December 8, 1986, marked the start of my inevitable journey though grief, one that continues still. You never cross a finish line in a journey like this, perhaps because it takes you in so many directions. It zigzags, climbs, descends, pulls and pushes. It's more of a verb than a noun.

For months after that horrible afternoon, I couldn't walk that same sidewalk, I turned my head every time Mercy Hospital came into view and the sight of a steaming bowl of chili could make me cry.

Eight months before he became ill, in a journal he kept, Jim wrote about his excitement at landing the editing position at *The Sun*. He'd wanted the job for several years and, at forty, it finally was his.

"I have a feeling," he wrote, "that we're headed for a period in which our general happiness will be greater than it ever has been before. My new job, our new house, the summer coming—all these things contribute to a feeling of optimism and confidence that I'm almost afraid to express for fear it's false."

The night the doctors found the brain tumor, I left Jim in a hospital room that smelled like dirty diapers. The old man who had the other bed had been given a couple of enemas earlier and was hidden behind a green curtain. We didn't see him that night. We only heard him grunt. Before I left, Jim and I held one another and whispered like teenagers at curfew because it was almost midnight, we were in a hospital, and there was a sick man with bad bowels in the same room with us.

In this strange, new landscape, we assured each other everything would be fine. I tried to believe Jim and I wanted him to believe me. Why, then, did my heart feel dead?

Jim and I had been together three and a half years by then, and I'd worked for him as a reporter for a couple of years before that on a small daily newspaper in Hagerstown, Maryland. He was so gifted an editor that I scheduled my vacations to coincide with his because it wasn't the same newsroom without Jim Thomas in it. There was an ease and a grace about Jim that drew folks to him. He had an utter lack of self-consciousness and a laugh that still haunts me.

One hot summer night in June 1983, I asked Jim for a ride home. We were among the late-night stragglers in the newspaper's parking lot, the revered spot where the town's chroniclers gathered after the taverns closed. I slid onto the back of Jim's motorcycle, thrilled to be that close to him. He was married, happily I had thought. In fact, Jim was a mirror image of myself, restless and unsatisfied. He had kept a lot hidden and, together that night, we were like dry timber and fuel. All we had needed was the match.

Not long after that, Jim ended his first marriage and became a news editor in Baltimore at the now-defunct *News American*. Every moment I was apart from him seemed like a millennium and, a couple of months later, I quit my job, put Hagerstown in the rear-view and joined Jim in Baltimore. I was twenty-seven, never-married, crazy in love, and scared to death.

In those first, startling months, in the quiet of our attic apartment, Jim and I comforted one another, confided in one another, laughed at one another. There was nothing about me he did not know. Neither of us ever looked back because the present was so full.

In time, Jim's first wife crafted a new life for herself, later remarrying. As the sun rose over our rowhouse in Baltimore on December 8, 1986, Jim's daughters, Anne, then fifteen, and eighteen-year-old Aimée were getting ready for classes twenty miles away in the townhouse they shared with their mother. At that point, Anne was a regular at our place on weekends, and Aimée was just starting to carve out a niche for herself in the household. We were beginning to feel like a family.

"Brain tumor. Brain tumor. Oh, Jesus, brain tumor," I recited to myself as I drove home from the hospital that first night. The words curled in my mouth and stung my tongue. We had been married exactly a year and a half. I'd given Jim an anniversary card that same wintry morning and teased him about wearing my corduroys. We had a similar build, only his was longer. Alone in bed that night, I sang myself to sleep: "Happy anniversary to you."

It was several days before anyone at the hospital said the word "cancer." The doctors, so businesslike and impersonal, seemed to think the tumor was operable. They reminded me of most mechanics I've known: I felt completely at their mercy, I almost instinctively questioned their honesty, and I couldn't help wondering whether they were going to deliver what they said they were. The doctors were heartened by Jim's age and relative fitness, but they advised him to write a will "just in case."

I don't know what's more frightening—the unknown or knowing too much. The strongest drug Jim was taking those first few days was Tylenol with codeine. How sick could he be? Sure, the nurses took a daily sputum sample from him, but we thought of it as spit-up, not as a host for cancer cells. At the time, the concept of a brain tumor was so foreign that it seemed unreal, at most a temporary visitor. We still didn't know enough about what was eating away at Jim's insides to scare us.

Everything changed on December 14 when we learned

about the tumor in his lung. It was the primary tumor and it had spun off cancer cells to the brain and the bones. Jim's body was riddled with the stuff. Diagnosis: lung cancer.

Jim had stopped smoking three months earlier, saying he was tired of feeling beaten-up. He had smoked a pack or so a day for twenty years. In fact, he has a cigarette in his hand in just about every photograph I have of him. It was part of his signature. As the doctor explained the diagnosis in measured monotone, I could still taste Marlboro Light on my own rank breath, my tongue darting the length of my lips in hideous reflex. I had smoked for fifteen years without ever having tried to stop, but that day I quit for good.

As the doctor continued to talk, I sat on the edge of the trim hospital bed, staring blindly at the large wooden crucifix in the sterile hallway outside Jim's room. I can't remember now what the doctor looked like or even what he said. I only remember what I felt—forsaken, alone and strangely short of breath. It seemed like the air had been sucked out of the room. I tried to listen but unbidden images kept distracting me. I couldn't stop imagining the hungry tumors that were multiplying beneath Jim's skin.

That night, I prayed like hell. I lay on my back, stared at the ceiling and prayed to God to please let Jim live. "Oh God, dear God." The words stuck in my throat. I felt caught in a terrible transaction between Jim and God and I was self-conscious about praying. It was something I did only when I was desperate, yet this hardly seemed an unreasonable request. All I wanted was for everything to stay the same. That's all I was asking for. "Dear God, please God."

I bargained, I begged, and finally I wept so hard I

held a pillow over my mouth to muffle the sound of my cries. I was afraid our neighbors would hear me screaming.

A few days before Christmas, the doctors ruled out surgery because the tumors were so widespread, discharging Jim with a treatment plan that included radiation and chemotherapy. "I feel like I've been expelled for bad behavior," Jim muttered as he packed up his hospital bag. "Let's go home."

A loneliness had entered our house in Jim's absence. The milk he bought in large, plastic jugs had soured in the refrigerator. His side of the closet hadn't been budged open in almost two weeks and our bed had seemed lopsided without his weight on the other side. We had never spent so many nights apart. A few afternoons later, as we slid under the cool sheets, I pressed my lips against the places we knew the tumors had lodged: Jim's head, pelvis, shoulder and ribs. We believed that if we made love, we would regain our balance and, at least in the privacy of those moments, banish the cancer from our sanctuary.

"In sickness and in health." In my mind, I kept hearing those words, and I might even have said them aloud. I wanted to be touched so much my skin tingled, the way it always does after I've had too much sun. Jim's body felt the same to me, a little thinner, but it didn't feel the same to him. How could it? It had been loaded with painkillers, zapped by radiation and invaded by disease. For the next forty-five minutes, I held Jim close and rocked him until, finally, he slept. When he woke up several hours later, the room that had been caressed by narrow strips of pale afternoon light had darkened to black, as if a flame had been extinguished. It was the last time we ever tried to make love.

On Christmas, I prepared Beef Wellington, a beef dish wrapped in pastry that was one of Jim's favorites. Trying to pretend there was nothing unusual happening, I fumbled with the dough I'd bought in an Italian gourmet shop on the west side of town. It was gummy and unruly, thicker than it should have been. I'd followed the directions, but the Beef Wellington was shaping up into a disaster. I wasn't much of a cook. That had always been Jim's job—and joy. I was only trying to replicate the Christmas dinner he had made the year before. I wanted desperately to cling to the ordinary. But nothing was familiar and everything was extraordinary.

The day before Christmas, I had driven Jim to the radiation oncologist's for a morning treatment and by afternoon I was in a crowd of excited holiday shoppers at Baltimore's Lexington Market, where I had gone to pick up the fat fillet I had special-ordered for the Beef Wellington. The loud throng of jubilant shoppers only seemed to underscore my own isolation. Looking at their happy, expectant faces, I fought the urge to slap them. After paying the butcher $24, I ran out of the market, aimed the car at the holiday traffic and stopped at a liquor store on the way home for a couple of cold six-packs. I was beginning to discover that even in the context of dying, the ordinary demands of life do not diminish: You still get stuck in traffic and you still run out of beer.

The radiation treatments took place in a doctor's office, where we'd see the same patients every day, mostly old people or women with breast cancer. Somehow, their tragedies seemed worse than ours. In the waiting room, under a poster that advised "Eat! Eat! Eat!," folks talked amicably about food tolerance, vitamins, pain medication and, sometimes, the sorry specifics of their disease. I tried to shut out their voices, burying my face in a magazine in the farthest corner of the room. I felt safer that way. It wasn't the kind of place where I wanted to stand out. I didn't want to be one of them.

During radiation therapy, which spanned five long weeks, Jim was treated for "hot spots"—a much nicer word than cancer—in his head, his pelvic area, his ribs and his shoulder. The technicians marked the field of radiation in purple ink. Before long, Jim's body looked like a road map. At home with Jim at night, I would follow the lines with my fingers, then my lips. But this wasn't the sort of hurt that a kiss could make better.

On New Year's Eve, we finally had something to celebrate. "New pain medication regimen cut pain in half overnight," Jim noted in the appointment calendar he kept by the bed. "Slept through night for the first time in two weeks." The tumors had begun to press up against his nerves and bones, and though sleep was to become elusive and the pain unimaginable, he rarely complained. By the end of January, a tumor had pushed against a rib, snapping it like a matchstick.

Years later, one of the oncologists told me Jim had the most aggressive form of non-small cell lung cancer he had ever seen in terms of its relentless attack on the bones and the rapidity of its spread.

But in those early days of the disease, our hearts were filled with hope and nobody talked about dying. On faded yellow notepaper, in my sister Barbara's girlish handwriting, are the questions we concerned ourselves with at the time: 1) Is there still a chance of surgery after radiation? 2) When will we be able to tell if the disease has been arrested? 3) How do you avoid hurting the good cells? 4) If it was you, Doctor, what would you do?

Barbie, six years my junior, shared a house with Jim and me. I may have been the engine that kept the household running in those numbing weeks, but she was the fuel. I looked after Jim and she looked after me. The day we found out about the lung tumor, Barbie and I sat at the old pine table in our living room as she read aloud the lengthy entry on lung cancer from her medical encyclopedia.

"A respiratory disorder attributable to cigarette smoking in seventy-five percent of cases," she began reading. "Surgery is the most effective treatment, but only one-half of the cases can be treated by surgery by the time this disease is detected. Lung cancer is usually far advanced when detected and spreads widely to other organs."

Barbie told me a couple of years later that she had recited everything that long, dark night except for the survival rate. To herself, she had read silently, "Less than ten percent of lung cancer patients survive five years after diagnosis. If the cancer has spread beyond the chest, a cure is highly unlikely."

Months earlier, at the beginning of 1986, Jim wrote letters to me almost every day as a way to stay close when work assignments kept us apart. Reading those letters now from the perch of distance, I've fallen in love with Jim all over again. The memory is like a preservative, molding the contours of our lives, but letters deliver the long forgotten details, the hidden pieces of a heart.

Sometimes two and three pages, the letters would show up marked "personal" with my mail at the office. Writing to me on the day his daughter Aimée turned eighteen, Jim reflected, "I don't want to lose Aimée— ever. I think she needs me. And I know that, somehow, I need her too." On the subject of growing older, a discourse prompted by my 30th birthday, he noted, "When speaking of getting older, I've always said I have the eerie feeling that I either have missed or am going to miss something. Missing what? I'm almost always not sure, but I'm determined not to let time get away without at least considering the question and looking for answers."

In several of the letters, Jim discusses his growing passion for motorcycle racing, which had become the metaphor for his life—and, in a way, for my own. Sometimes, I think he was happiest on the track, the one place he felt closest to personal freedom.

"I have it in me, I know, if not to win at least to try," Jim wrote the summer before the diagnosis. "I spent a lot of years settling for survival and comfort and taking the easy way out. When you do that you don't have to try very hard. But I know now I am made to try as hard as I can. There's no satisfaction otherwise. Everybody should have at least one element of their lives that pushes back the boundaries, that shows they can transcend what they thought were their limits. It's more than just thrill-seeking. It's proving there's more out there to see and do and feel…. In a big way, racing has become almost a symbol of how much my life has changed. I'm gaining control, I'm gaining knowledge and I'm gaining confidence. And I'm learning that my talents are greater than I ever thought possible."

Question No. 5 on the list of inquiries we presented to the doctors at the start of radiation, this one written in Jim's scrawl, asked: "Ride bike?"

*   *   *   *   *   *   *   *

Two weeks into the radiation therapy, on a morning in early January, I woke up with a clump of Jim's brown hair in my mouth. "Oh my God, Jim!" I screamed as I scooped a handful of his hair from my pillowcase. "Your hair. It's all over the bed." Wide awake now, Jim's hands went reflexively to his head, which looked like an unevenly mowed lawn. He refused to go to the mirror at first so I sat next to him, examining the bald spots and combing the loosened hair, which clung to the teeth of Jim's blue comb like pine needles caught in a rake.

"Stop it," Jim shouted finally, hobbling like an old man into the bathroom to survey himself in the mirror above the sink. I think he was frightened by what he saw—a face that was beginning to wear a chiseled, haunted look; bald patches where the day before hair had been; and a complexion that had turned oily and slick from the radiation and drugs. "I don't look like me anymore," Jim concluded. "Where did I go?"

I had always loved the look of Jim—the pitch of his thigh as he straddled his motorcycle; the way he'd crouch like a baseball catcher and rock back and forth on his heels; the smile slung across a face that was lived-in, but gentle, and the low, soothing voice that curled and slid across words like an old blues singer's.

But in those few weeks, Jim had lost so much weight that his jeans billowed on him and his weakened legs were beginning to lose their muscle tone. Walking had become difficult and, on bad days, he winded easily, his breath sneaking out in short, choppy gasps. He wasn't even strong enough to kick-start his bike. Every time I looked at Jim, there was a little less of him.

I don't know when I realized that Jim was dying, if there was one illuminated instant when I glimpsed the future or if it was knowledge that steeped inside me until recognition finally dawned. But then, recognition and acknowledgment are two different things. Mostly, I busied myself worrying about how the disease was affecting other people—Jim himself, his daughters, our parents. It was an almost automatic response and certainly one that was less painful than dredging my own heart.

Shortly after Jim was diagnosed, we began to see a counselor. Ralph Schwartz was his name. After a counseling session with us in late January, Ralph noted in his client log: "Jim asked doctors all the right questions except for how much time he has left. Ellen and Jim want to make the most of the time they have left together, however long that may be." By unspoken agreement, Jim and I stopped talking about the future. The most painful sound I knew was the ticking of a clock.

In the newsroom, when I managed to get there, I tired quickly and I couldn't seem to focus. I didn't tell Jim that I'd started crying mid-sentence during a story interview, the tears surprising me with their ferocity. At times, I sought refuge in the bathroom stall near my desk. I'd press my hands against my mouth, hoping to stifle the sobs, hiding behind the locked door until I regained control of my breathing. A few people at work had begun to avert their eyes when I walked by and, if they did look at me, it was with a mixture of sympathy, curiosity and sometimes pity. Some even asked what I would do after Jim was "gone," as if he was a weather pattern passing in the night. I felt like I had a neon badge on my jacket: "Wife of cancer patient." I don't suppose I masked my feelings well.

"She's strong, very strong, and optimistic," Jim wrote in his journal. "But I have seen and sensed that she has lots of tears ready to flow and they're waiting just below the surface. One major prompt from me and she will break down. I don't want to be the cause of that right now. I fear there will be too much opportunity for that later."

Business editor Phil Moeller, my boss, was very kind, letting me wrap my work schedule around the steadily increasing medical demands. In mid-January, Phil dispatched me to New York on assignment, suggesting it would be good for me to get away for a few days. I'm glad he did. The story I'd been sent to cover wasn't taxing and I relished my nights alone in a city where I could be completely anonymous. I could almost forget my husband had cancer. I caught up on the bills, wrote belated Christmas cards and ordered room service.

But there was no hiding from Jim's cancer. On January 26, less than two months after the diagnosis, Jim made this notation in his journal:

"I'm starting to cry a lot these past few days, sometimes uncontrollably... I think I'm getting a firmer and firmer grip on what's actually happening to me... I seldom can give a reason for the tears and, often, in the middle of a crying spell, I find myself pushing a bit to keep the tears flowing. Sometimes, I know what I'm crying about, though. Mostly it goes like this: I see myself lying on the bed dying (sometimes peacefully, sometimes painfully). I think of Ellen and how little time we had together and how much more time we will miss. Then I think of Aimée and Anne, floating adrift already, but even more in trouble because I'm not there anymore. A line from an old Bukka White blues song says it all better than I can: 'Lord, I don't mind dying, but I hate to see my children crying'."

As we went into February, it seemed we had never known anything but the cancer, so connected were we to it. Time developed a sharpness. Moments somehow seemed larger. We were weighted in the present in a landscape that, while unfamiliar and disquieting, had a depth that was extraordinarily vivid and illuminative. As we searched our hearts for understanding, we discovered a simple sweetness to life, a holiness almost. I have never felt closer to a human being than I did to Jim during those months.

After our third counseling session in mid-February, the social worker, Ralph, added this note to our file: "Jim is in chemotherapy now but realizes the cancer is spreading. He is trying to take care of himself and do things for Ellen. He's keeping a positive attitude but anger is coming out. He is very frustrated with his body changes, the way he's losing control of his 'self'."

The one good thing about chemotherapy was that it put us in touch with the doctor who would become our chief oncologist, Jon Minford, a soft-spoken man a few years younger than Jim. Three of Dr. Minford's four grandparents had died of cancer by the time he turned ten, and he has devoted his professional life to helping relieve the kind of suffering he witnessed as a child. The last time I saw Dr. Minford alone, he cried because he had not been able to help us. Much later, he was to tell me: "If I had to see a patient like Jim every week, I couldn't do this."

On chemo days, Jim sat in a recliner in the doctor's office and took the drugs in his arm through an IV tube.

The chemotherapy threw Jim into a strange sleep, a stupor of sorts. He talked a lot while he was sleeping but I could never understand what he said and he could never remember. Sitting beside him, I'd put my ear to his mouth, trying to figure out what his ramblings meant. I kept thinking he had something important to say.

One afternoon on the way to a chemotherapy session, the Plymouth blew a tire on a highway ramp and almost immediately a young man stopped to help us. "Oh, thank you," I said, pointing to Jim who was sitting in the car. "My husband's sick and we're on our way to a doctor's appointment." Further explanation seemed unnecessary. The stranger changed the tire effortlessly, then asked what was wrong with Jim. "Cancer," I said, and the man started to cry. I felt so sorry for him. Then he wished us good luck and drove away. I will never forget his face when the tears came.

At times, it seemed like Jim had turned into another person. It was as if a stranger had moved into his body. The Jim I knew could have fixed that tire. Then there was his coffee cup. He drank his coffee black and he drank it all day. This new person didn't like the taste of coffee, couldn't even stand the aroma. I never drink coffee, but I deeply missed the reassuring sight of Jim's stained coffee cup in the kitchen sink.

A few weeks into February, Jim and I took the train to New York to visit his brother, Jeff, and his girlfriend, Jenny, a Korean musician. Jim hadn't had chemotherapy or radiation for almost two weeks and he was feeling reasonably well. One afternoon, Jim and Jenny went to an Asian doctor Jenny knew about to buy a special blend of tea that was supposed to cure just about anything. I think there was tree bark, a fungus and some sort of antler in the rich, black blend, which cost $150. When Jim returned to our hotel room that evening, he unwrapped the newspaper that the tea was bound in and reverently displayed it as if it was treasure. When we got back to Baltimore, I cooked the tea for seven hours, just as the doctor had said. It smelled awful but Jim was confident it was going to do him some good, and periodically he'd walk into the kitchen to check on its progress. That evening, as both my sister and I watched, Jim took one sip and threw up. A few days later, he gathered what remained of his precious tea and threw it in the trash. Jenny, who was so moved by Jim's suffering, died of ovarian cancer two years later.

Until Jim became ill, I had never dealt with doctors and over the months they were transformed in my mind from life-giving gods to mere mortals. I had never even spent the night in a hospital until I stayed overnight with Jim in one. From almost the beginning, we sought to accept the cancer as part of our lives. We tried to understand it and, on some level, we even tried to please it. What else could we do? Wish it away? It would have been easier to pull the moon from the sky.

It was far more difficult to accept the daily diminishments that Jim had to endure. The lost hair. The lost weight. The broken ribs. The weakness that gutted his strength and caused him to seek the support of a cane and then a walker and then a wheelchair. Every day, the cancer claimed another piece of him. We clung to the small victories to sustain us.

Jim woke up in great pain on March 11. He kept gasping for air and clutching his chest. "We've got to get you to the emergency room," I demanded, ordering the fear from my voice. My heart was pounding. Jim was racked with pain, worse than any before. "No hospitals," he pleaded, choking on the words. "Just be a minute. Be OK in a minute. No hospitals."

I know Jim felt his body had betrayed him. He kept apologizing, as if this was all his fault. Finally, he agreed we needed help. Driving back to Mercy Hospital that morning, we both felt like failures.

Jim was hospitalized again—this time for eleven days. A woman we knew only casually visited Jim in the hospital one day at lunch. She inquired about his health, offered the usual niceties and then asked the unimaginable: "How long, Jim?"

Jim had decided early on that he didn't want to know how long the doctors expected him to live. As a matter of principle, he had never believed in absolutes and the notion that a physician would tell him when he was going to die was repugnant to him. I joined Jim in that decision. Willful ignorance, I called it. Others might call it denial.

During the time he was home between the two hospitalizations, Jim watched a movie on the VCR called *Tribute*. In it, Jack Lemmon plays a Broadway agent who is diagnosed with terminal cancer. "You know the weird thing?" Lemmon says to his ex-wife after his doctor tells him how ill he is. "I don't resent dying. What bothers me is knowing when. I guess somehow it robs the event of all its spontaneity."

As I was leaving the hospital one night, a nurse whom I'd grown fond of stopped me in the hallway outside Jim's room. She took my hand, searched my face with her sad green eyes, and said, "You're so young. I'm so sorry."

No doctor could have given a clearer prognosis.

CHAPTER
2

THE PASSAGE THROUGH HOPE

Even as the cancer spun its web tighter and tighter around us, we sought to disengage ourselves from it. On the day Jim was discharged from Mercy Hospital, we flew west, to the place writer Wallace Stegner calls "Hope's native home."

It's strange how in those first months of the illness the meanings of so many words turned completely around for me, words like "marriage" and "husband" and "health." Their solid definitions collapsed into a hodgepodge of letters. They became unreliable. They couldn't even hold up a sentence.

"Hope," on the other hand, expanded into something textured and real, a shoulder to cushion me from contact that was too painful, a net to break my fall. If hope wouldn't come to us, then we would go to it. "The paper posted the job today for the West Coast news bureau," I said to Jim one night after work in January.

"Why don't you apply?"

I shrugged. "Right."

The job was out of reach. Any move now was out of the question. But the notion of moving to San Francisco stirred something in Jim and we spent most of that evening playing, "What if?" Jim thought of every reason we should make such a move and I thought of every reason we shouldn't. Somehow, "What if?" turned into "Why not?" and minutes before the deadline for applications closed a few days later, I added my name to the list of candidates.

I figured I wasn't in any danger of getting the job. I wasn't even sure I wanted it. Besides, it was unlikely *The Baltimore Sun* would offer the coveted one-person bureau to a reporter whose husband was dying. I was wrong.

"We got it, Jim," I whispered, handing him a travel video about San Francisco that I'd rented on the way home after learning I'd won the assignment. In that moment, trouble left Jim's face. The dark half-moons under his eyes, the tense set of his jaw, the worry lines engraved between his brows—they all vanished.

Watching the video in our bedroom that night, we imagined ourselves dancing in the cool embrace of the famed fog, running at top-speed for a cable car and feeding on the feast of sensory pleasures the city promised. We imagined ourselves healthy. Even Jim's oncologist, Dr. Minford, was excited about the move. The medical center at the University of California in San Francisco is known for its work in cancer research and experimental drug therapy. "Cutting-edge," Dr. Minford called it. This really was hope's native home.

But by March, Jim was back in the hospital and I worried the move would be too much for him. In fact, day after day for almost a week, we had to delay our departure date because the doctors refused to discharge him. We felt like hostages to Jim's body. There was no denying he was frail. He couldn't sit in one position for more than a few minutes because of the pain, and the nausea had become unpredictable. Who were we kidding, anyway? How was Jim going to survive the long flight, with a layover in Chicago, let alone adapt to a completely new environment? I also felt guilty about putting an entire country between Jim and his daughters. Had we made a terrible mistake?

Years later, Anne told me, "He should have spent those months with me and Aimée. There was no closure. At the age I was, who was he to leave me? If only he'd said, 'Maybe I'm going to die,' instead of trying until the very last day to live. That's not blame or hate talking. It's sadness."

On March 21, a hospital volunteer loaded Jim into a wheelchair and pushed him outside onto the sidewalk in front of Mercy Hospital. After all the waiting and worrying, there was something sad and incomplete about Jim's release. Isn't a person supposed to feel reasonably OK when he leaves a hospital? Well, Jim didn't. His body looked lost inside baggy sweatpants, a red San Francisco T-shirt and my jean jacket. He was so thin I was afraid a gust of March wind would carry him away. In my mind, I actually pictured that happening.

"You look great," I told Jim.

"Compared to what?" At least he hadn't lost his sense of humor.

My sister picked us up in the faithful Plymouth, our suitcases already stowed in its trunk. I had been packed for days just waiting for the doctors to sign the discharge papers. While Jim was in the hospital, the movers had packed up the house and I had said my goodbyes. Barbie drove us directly to the airport and, in a matter of fifteen miles, Baltimore was behind us. Barbie was convinced that morning she would never see Jim again. As she said goodbye, she cradled her head in his shoulder and felt his warmth. For the rest of that day, I learned later, she imagined Jim dead.

As our plane soared west, I thought of all we had left:

Jim's daughters, our closest friends, the house we'd bought just the year before, my old green Plymouth, the motorcycles, the newsroom, the sum of almost four years together. But we were traveling toward something we had begun to lose sight of in Baltimore: hope. It filled us with purpose and pushed us forward. It felt good to be in motion again.

We spent that first week near Los Angeles at my parents' house in Rancho Palos Verdes, where we had married. I know it pained my parents to be near us, to catch glimpses of Jim's demons and to imagine my own. Walking outside the floor-to-ceiling window of the guest room one afternoon, I looked in at where Jim was resting. He was kneeling over the bed as if in prayer, his arms outstretched and his face bunched tight like a balled fist. In the privacy of his torment, the despair moved unguarded across his face. He never knew I saw him and, when he emerged from the bedroom an hour later, Jim enthusiastically reported to my mother what a restful nap he had enjoyed.

Looking through the window that day, I wanted to jump inside his body and trade places with him. On that afternoon, I stopped crying for me and started crying for him.

As the illness grabbed hold, the weeks lost definition. There were no Mondays or Fridays. There were simply good days and bad days. On one very good day, my parents and Jim and I ferried over to Santa Catalina, a small craggy island that rises above the Pacific twenty-six miles off the California coast. The pain pills were doing their job and Jim was in an expansive mood. He felt so buoyant on the boat ride that he drank a Bloody Mary, the first alcohol he had touched in months.

"To vacations," Jim said as he held up his glass.

There is something thrilling to me about an island, even if it is a place I know, and that morning as we pushed off the pier I felt like an adventurer and Catalina seemed like the Promised Land.

The four of us explored the tiny streets of Avalon, the island's quaint and only town, and then ate huge Cobb salads soaked in poppy seed dressing at the Busy Bee, a popular waterfront restaurant. Afterward, we rode a bus through the mountains where we saw wildflowers clinging delicately to cliffs, a few wandering buffalo imported there years ago for a Western movie shoot and an emerald cove so heartbreakingly beautiful it made me cry. Sometimes, the land does that to me. Until Jim became ill, I never cried much. Ever since, I have tried to listen closely to what my tears are saying.

Walking through town, Jim leaned against me, taking my arm as he grew tired. I had begun to feel that my body was an extension of his. It was an intimacy, potent and deep, that transcends even the sort shared by lovers. At times, I did not know where I ended and he began.

For me, Catalina is as much a state of mind as a place, and on that spring day it gave us its greatest gift: each other. It was the closest we had come to our old selves since the diagnosis.

Toward the end of March, feeling renewed, we headed up the coast, eager to meet Jim's new oncologist. The first appointment was scheduled April 2.

"I'll drive," Jim said, sliding behind the wheel of the 1976 Nova we had purchased a few days earlier. The car was over ten years old and only had 15,000 miles on it. It also had comfortable, padded seats that seemed to soothe the soreness in Jim's back. He had become so

thin and bony that prolonged contact with any surface
caused discomfort.

Automatically, I had walked to the driver's side, as I
had done since Jim first became sick. It felt good to
hand over the controls. My father said later he had
worried about Jim driving because of all the medication
he was taking. He had seen Jim's toiletry kit, which
housed a small pharmacy. But neither Dad nor I sought
to dissuade him. It seemed cruel to do so. He had been
stripped of so much already.

As we cleared Los Angeles, Jim's new key chain, a
blue plastic ring with a picture of the old casino at
Catalina, clicked against the ignition. Jim had lost so
much weight that his wedding band kept sliding off his
finger and during the drive he unceremoniously installed
his ring on the key chain.

"Will you wear a wedding ring?" I had asked Jim a
couple of months before we married.

"No," he said. "Not unless it means something to
you."

I thought about all the rituals I disliked about
weddings, the patterns that irritated me about so many
marriages. Then I looked at Jim. "It means something."

We bought the ring for $50 at one of those big catalog
stores on the way to get our blood test for the marriage
license. Except for when he was working on his
motorcycles, he'd always worn it.

Click, click.

As Jim's key chain bounced against the ignition, I
twisted my own ring around my finger in short, circular
motions, watching his and saying nothing.

We spent that night at the El Rey, a roadside motel
not far from the Hearst castle in San Simeon. It was the

night of the 1987 Academy Awards. We were so accustomed to Eastern Standard Time that we marveled at the fact that you could watch the Oscars on television and still be in bed by 9:30. There was a whirlpool tub in our room and Jim spent most of the night in it. His bones had started to ache again.

The next morning we toured the opulent coastal retreat built by newspaper mogul William Randolph Hearst. All three walking tours were physically challenging, even the "easy" one we took. The castle was remarkable, but the thing I remember most about that day was that it was pretty much the last time Jim walked.

Everything changed after we left San Simeon. As I drove the narrow, winding Pacific Coast Highway toward Carmel, Jim sat hunched over in the back seat, his eyes clamped shut, his face plowed with pain. I tried to ignore him, preferring the serenity of the shoreline to the sight of the sick man in my rear-view mirror.

"Open your eyes and enjoy the goddamn ride," I screamed finally, adding a silent postscript: "You'll never see this again."

I wanted to tell Jim that I was scared, that fear had burrowed so deep in my gut I couldn't even find it. I wanted to ask, "Are you afraid of dying? What does it feel like?" I wanted to say, "How dare you leave me now!" I wanted to know: Would he miss me? But all I could do was yell and all he could do was weep.

The cancer was like a second skin, a shadow we couldn't shake. In a way, I was jealous because there were times when Jim seemed closer to it than to me. We had always been able to talk to each other but, with the cancer wedged between us, I choked on the words I most wanted to say. I was afraid that if I started to talk I wouldn't be able to stop. I drove into a scenic overlook and crawled into the back seat with Jim. He popped a couple of pain pills and I took his hand. His body was trembling. I have never felt more ashamed.

My parents had made reservations for us at the Lamplighter Inn in Carmel. They had booked the Bluebird Room, the same room where they had honeymooned thirty-two years earlier. A bottle of chilled champagne was waiting for us in the suite. "Nice touch," I thought, until I opened the card attached to the bottle: "Welcome Honeymooners! Compliments of the Management."

Someone at the front desk had made a mistake. The irony wasn't lost on me. My parents had been here at the start of their marriage. I was here at the end of mine. I drank the entire bottle of champagne while Jim dozed on couch cushions next to the bed. The mattress was soft and lumpy and it had made his back only feel worse. Before I went to bed, I called my sister to wish her a happy 25th birthday.

"How is he?" she asked.

"Fine," I lied. "We're both just fine."

I went to sleep a few hours later with my arm dangling off the bed, my hand reaching out for Jim's. From a painting above the bed, a bluebird of happiness kept watch over us that night.

*   *   *   *   *   *   *   *

If you look at a map of San Francisco, you will find Grandview Avenue at its center. We pulled in front of our stucco apartment house on April Fool's Day and climbed the four flights to the spacious, two-story apartment, which had been occupied by my predecessor in *The Sun's* West Coast bureau. It was the only time Jim was able to climb the stairs, and then just barely. It took him nearly twenty minutes. The next time he would have to be carried.

Jim couldn't believe that the apartment was ours. Even unfurnished, it looked glorious. The landlord always refers to it as the penthouse, but I could never bring myself to call it that. Too pretentious. But it is lovely— open, airy and white, and there are windows at every turn, ushering in thick layers of warm afternoon light. We were in the middle of a city but out back is a country garden with roses, calalilies and an orange flower I especially like called the enchantment lily. The best part of the house is its view, a spectacular expanse that stretches clear across the spires of downtown San Francisco and unfolds over the bay past Oakland. At about three o'clock on most afternoons, the fog creeps in like a cat and turns everything a filmy white, then at night the lights assert themselves and sparkle like so many diamonds against a black-velvet sky. In that magical moment, surveying the view from the rooftop deck, Jim and I felt like the two luckiest people on earth.

We booked a room that night at the Roberts Motel, an inexpensive seaside inn next to a diner run by an old Armenian who makes the best omelettes in San Francisco. Every morning, the Armenian's crusty pals huddle at the gray Formica counter, drinking black coffee and fouling the air with their smoke. I watched them while I waited for carry-out to take back to the room. I liked the way they seemed to belong together.

Jim didn't sleep well that first night in San Francisco

and we made our way the next morning to the oncologist's office in hopes of a wonder drug. On some level, I think I expected one. Folks at the university medical center were nice enough to us, but the hospital hardly seemed the sort where cutting-edge research was taking place. Jim was just another patient whose body needed to be weighed, whose blood needed to be taken, whose insurance information needed to be recorded.

On April 3, just before daybreak, Jim nudged me awake. He was burning with fever and the sheets were soaked. I helped him to the car and we raced up Judah Street toward the hospital at eighty miles per hour on the elevated roadway reserved for the municipal railway. There's a sign on just about every corner warning motorists to "Stay Off Ramp." I kept wondering what I'd tell a cop if we were stopped. We decided to go directly to the oncology department, bypassing the emergency room because we feared a delay in treatment there. Within moments of our arrival, a nurse injected Jim with the painkiller Demerol. He was admitted to the hospital a few hours later for what the doctors politely called "pain management." He wasn't released until twenty-five days later, on April 28, his 41st birthday.

Isn't it strange how we all start off thinking we can plan the way our lives will turn out? Four months earlier, I hadn't known what "oncology" meant. I didn't even know how to spell it. I was looking forward to Christmas and, in the spring, planting a garden behind our Baltimore rowhouse. But here it was spring and I was alone in Room No. 4 of a cheap motel, drinking a beer and thinking about a husband dying.

* * * * * * * *

Slowly, distractedly, I began to build my life, our lives, in San Francisco. The day after Jim was hospitalized, the movers arrived and my father drove up from Los Angeles to help me unpack. Aunts and uncles from Sacramento showed up and painted the kitchen, papered the bathroom and helped me hang window blinds and pictures.

"Where do you want me to hang your motorcycle plaques?" I asked Jim about the half-dozen or so plaques he had won racing. "How do you think I ought to position the dressers?" The questions were silly but I wanted Jim to feel he had a life outside the hospital. I tried to share the whole of my days with him—the telephone conversations I had with people back at the newsroom in Baltimore, discoveries I'd made in the new neighborhood, what I'd eaten for lunch. His world had grown so small—the size of a hospital room and the view from a window. I wanted to enlarge it for him.

Outside of Jim's room, on the eleventh floor of the Long Annex, stood a barren hillside, and above it stretched the orange and white Mount Sutro tower, a broadcast tower that presides over the city. I could see the same tower from our bedroom, two miles away. Every night, from our separate rooms, we would gaze at the tower and whisper, "Goodnight." It is only a metal tower, I know, but for me it will always be the sacred sentry that kept us safe while we slept. I call it Jim's Tower.

I filed a few stories for *The Sun*, though not many, while Jim was in the hospital. I stayed with him as often as I could, sometimes sleeping overnight on the sticky vinyl couch in his room. We watched TV, read the papers

and got to know the guts of the eleventh floor: We
learned which nurses gave the best needle sticks; which
patients were waiting for bone marrow transplants (there
were three); and which doctors were courageous enough
to be compassionate. I liked the hospital.

There was an openness of spirit that had been missing
at Mercy Hospital. The nurses even dressed differently.
In Baltimore, they had all worn conservative white
uniforms, but in San Francisco they wore white trousers
or skirts with colorful tops. It's a small thing, but it
made the whole place seem less sick. The nurses also made
me feel less of an outsider. One night, when Jim spiked a
fever, a nurse showed me how to wrap ice cubes in a sheet
and position them around his groin and under his armpits
to bring his temperature down. The next time his
temperature jumped, I was able to do it myself.

During April, the hospital became the center of
everything we knew and hoped for. A part of me felt
like I was betraying Jim every time I walked outside into
the sunshine. The world had started to look different:
Colors were richer, the landscape fuller, the air fresher.
A part of me yearned to get out, to walk unencumbered,
to soak in a world that wasn't governed by nursing shifts,
medication schedules and doctors' rounds.

Jim was released into the care of a home hospice
program on April 28. His parents had just flown in from
San Antonio for a visit and he was getting a blood
transfusion when they walked into the hospital room
that day.

"Happy birthday, Jimmy," his folks declared in unison.
It didn't matter how old he was, "Jimmy" is what they
always called Jim, and even now it is the young boy
who visits their memories first:

Jimmy, at eleven-and-a-half months, his first tentative steps leading him into the bathroom where his daddy is shaving. Jimmy at four pretending he's a captain fighting in the Korean War. And, later, Jimmy skipping rocks in a mountain stream in the Black Forest. Jimmy in a white coat and black tie, driving Shari Whitaker to the junior prom in his metallic green 1962 Nash Rambler Ambassador. Jimmy breaking his arm at high school football practice.

"Ah, Jimmy, you're heavier than the last time I carried you," said his father, also a Jim, as he helped the paramedics carry his oldest son and namesake up to the bedroom. The only San Francisco Jim ever really saw was framed by the windows on our top floor. I am thankful that the views were so lovely.

The hospice program assigned a nurse, physical therapist and social worker to our case, but basically I was to be the primary caregiver. "Caregiver" is one of those terms like "pain management," "skin integrity" and "bowel program" that becomes a part of your household lexicon when you're taking care of someone who's dying.

To celebrate Jim's birthday and homecoming, his mother, Gloria, prepared a pasta dinner that we carried upstairs to our room. I lit white candles in a French crystal candleholder, one of our wedding gifts, while Jim sprawled out like a king on crisp, new sheets. He was still bald, but his face had sprouted a thick, brown mustache and goatee, something he had never been able to grow before chemotherapy and radiation. He had taken off his shirt and I could see the ribs pushing against his skin, the purple radiation marker on his right shoulder and his new appendage: a clear, plastic tube that extended from a vein in his upper left chest to a gray metal hand-held device that automatically infused morphine at set intervals.

I turned the light off in the room as Gloria brought in the chocolate cake she had made for Jim. As we sang "Happy Birthday," I wanted to disappear into the undemanding darkness.

"Happy birthday to you. Happy birthday to you...."

Could the others, I wondered, hear the pounding of my heart, sense the despair in my voice, see the tears I fought to hold back?

"Happy birthday, dear Jimmy...."

Happy birthday? It took everything in me not to run out of the room.

"Happy birthday to you."

As the song drew to a close, his mother urged him to make a wish. But what do you wish for when you're about to lose everything? It was in that full, heavy moment that I began to say goodbye to Jim. I knew he would never live to see forty-two. What was left? Weeks? Months? It's odd how there had come to be such a familiarity to all of this, a sense that it would go on forever.

A couple of weeks earlier, I had ordered address labels with our two names and I had listed them both in the telephone book. I had even tried to put Jim's name on my new checking account, but the woman at the bank refused to do it without him present. I despised her for that. I wasn't ready to sever my connection with Jim, even if it was about something as trivial as our two names, printed side by side.

Every morning when he was in the hospital, the nurse asked Jim to name the president of the United States. It had gotten to be a bit of a joke. Of course, he knew who the president was. He could list them all.

"Abraham Lincoln," he had said a few days before he came home.

At first, I thought he was kidding.

"No?" His brown eyes registered surprise. Then he laughed.

I looked at him, silently willing him to say Reagan. "Go ahead, Jim. Tell her."

"Jimmy Carter?" There was unspeakable horror in Jim's eyes as we both began to understand that this hungry, hungry cancer could not be satiated. It wanted all of Jim.

Remarkably, Jim teased about his worsening condition, trying to shield me with humor. And when he ran out of words, he sought to comfort me with his hands and his eyes.

"I'm going to miss you so much," I told him a couple of weeks before he died. I was kneeling beside the bed, my brown hair hanging like tendrils of attachment over his face. It was hard to push the words out.

"I can't imagine what the world is going to be like without you in it." I tried to find a steady voice to speak in. "You are everything I ever wanted. I already miss you."

No more words would come. Jim pulled me close and rubbed his hand up and down the back of my head. Even in his darkest moments, he found it in himself to comfort me. Now, when I'm lonely sometimes, I think about Jim with his hand on my head. It is an image that always soothes me, and there have been times when I have thought I felt the warmth of his hand caressing me again.

I slept beside Jim that night with my lips pressed against his right temple and my arm draped across his waist. It had become our coupling position. I guess I figured that as long as I could wrap him within my body, he couldn't leave me. But, as he grew weaker, life and death became so blurred that I'd find myself holding my hand over his nose and mouth to make sure he was still breathing.

In the middle of every night during those last weeks, the alarm clock would shriek its wake-up call, shrilly ordering me downstairs to the kitchen. Stirring myself awake, I would grab a morphine syringe from the vegetable drawer in the refrigerator and walk back up to the bathroom to sterilize my hands. Then I'd remove the old syringe from its metal casing and replace it with the new one, making sure that the tubing was cleared of air bubbles.

One night after Jim first got home, I messed up. Blood backed up into the tube, something the nurses had warned me could be dangerous. I cut off the morphine for a couple of hours while I called various emergency numbers to try to figure out what to do. Finally, I got a nurse on the phone who calmly talked me through a tubing change. In the days after that, I changed tubing, replaced syringes, installed a catheter and dressed bed sores as if I had done it all my life.

I have always had a low threshold for pain, mine or anyone else's. When I was a kid, I ran away from the stove when my mother was frying bacon because I was afraid the grease would spatter and burn me. I couldn't stand to see someone else's cuts or sores and I wasn't comfortable around animals, even dogs, because I thought there was a chance they might hurt me. Yet, as I took care of Jim that last month, a calm settled over me. It seemed I could do anything—except save him.

A couple of days after Jim's birthday, an ambulance took him back to the hospital for a radiation treatment and an MRI, shorthand for magnetic resonance imaging. During an MRI, the patient is encased in a tube while a mix of electromagnets and radio waves produce detailed images of the body on a computer monitor. The MRI uncovered another tumor growing along Jim's spine.

By early May he had developed an insistent cough and was throwing up a lot. Visiting with my parents one day, I remember Jim would talk for a while and then politely cover his mouth and vomit into one of those yellow plastic pans they give you in hospitals. After collecting himself, he'd return to the conversation as if he had done something as ordinary as clearing his throat.

My father must have made the seven-hour drive from Los Angeles to San Francisco a half-dozen times that April and May, sometimes staying only a night. On one of those trips we gave him the wind chimes we had bought as a Father's Day present during our drive up to San Francisco. We knew it was unlikely Jim would live into June, so we gave them to Dad a month early, saying they were a thank-you gift for helping us settle in. On Father's Day, I told my dad what the true purpose of the chimes had been. By then, Jim had been dead three weeks.

My father loves those chimes and whenever I return to my parents' house, one of the first things I do is walk out back and listen to them. I always think of their song as Jim's voice.

*   *   *   *   *   *   *   *

Did you know you can have a 98.6-degree temperature and still be dying? Jim's temperature hovered close to normal throughout most of May although everything else about his body was wildly out of balance.

A typical day's nourishment consisted of a popsicle, a couple of glasses of iced tea, a bite of yogurt and a few cooked carrots. I hounded Jim like a drill sergeant to eat, but my presence at the bedroom door with yet another chocolate fudge pudding cup was clearly unwelcome.

"The Food Police," he'd say accusingly.

"Eat," I begged. "You've got to eat."

Jim would push his spoon around his plate. "I'm trying."

But, after awhile, he'd just ignore me, cutting off my entreaties with razor-sharp silence.

I had stocked the kitchen with pudding and fruit cups, variety packs of popsicles, apple sauce, chicken broth, JELL-O and Ensure, a high-calorie liquid drink. Food became a real issue, a power struggle that bloodied us both. Jim was frustrated he couldn't eat and I took his refusal to do so as a personal rebuke. We each felt we had failed the other. I wish now I had let up on him.

Nurses came by almost daily and for a time a physical therapist, Eileen Kotler, stopped in to help Jim "work out." On May 4, her first visit, she found muscle power in Jim's legs, feet and arms. Though he was very weak, he managed a few steps for Eileen that day with his walker.

"All right, Jim," I shouted. Four steps and we were elated. "That's fantastic." We had come to demand less and less of a "good day."

Up until a week before he died, Jim forced himself to use the walker or wheelchair at least once a day. He insisted on maneuvering himself from the bed to the wheelchair and moving unassisted into the next room, which I used as an office. For long stretches at a time, he'd gaze out the window, memorizing its view. Sometimes, he'd just sit and watch me work.

Jim was a fine editor and the few stories I wrote that May have a piece of him in them—a turn of phrase he had suggested or a restructured sentence. When I look at those stories now, the words that were his spring off the page like a secret code that draws me back to Jim.

On May 7, paramedics from King-American Ambulance Company collected Jim for what would be his final appointment with oncologists at the medical center. He is described in the terse transportation log as a "41-year-old male" suffering from "Ca/lungs." The impersonal shorthand reminded me of hundreds of police reports I've scanned over the years in search of a story. Seeing Jim described in the same generic terminology made me deeply sad, not for him but for me.

Dr. Alex Tseng, the oncologist, ushered us into his office. I didn't have to look at Jim's medical file to know the news was all bad. It was written all over Dr. Tseng's face.

"The disease is advancing rapidly," the young doctor said in hushed, apologetic tones.

I moved closer to Jim. His whole body seemed to have gone limp, the expression in his eyes concealed by half-closed lids.

"The tumors are growing and they're widespread." The doctor paused.

"There's nothing more we can do."

He warned Jim to drink a lot of liquids because his bones were disintegrating, creating high levels of calcium in the blood. Liquids would help dilute the calcium. I didn't realize as I pushed iced tea on Jim those next couple of weeks that blood loaded with calcium can shortcircuit the nervous system, causing dementia and coma.

Afterward, I wheeled Jim outside into the sun and we sat next to a flower bed, waiting for the ambulance to pick us up for the ride home.

"This could be the last time he's ever outdoors," I kept thinking as I waited for Jim to say something.

Finally, he spoke. "The only thing he didn't tell us was when."

I could hear Jim's thoughts echoing inside my own head.

"I'm still not interested in their projections. It will come soon enough, Ellen. I don't want to know when."

Jim propped my chin in his hand and studied my face.

"You're going to be OK," he promised. After that, I think, it was Jim who began to take care of me.

Later that day, after the paramedics had carried Jim upstairs, I rubbed olive oil on his head, which had begun to itch, and asked him to help me plan his funeral.

Over the months, Jim had set the tone for his dying. He had little patience for people whose own fears about death caused them to treat him with pity or alarm. I took my cues from Jim and when he decided he didn't want the doctors to tell him "how long," I stood by him.

In truth, I was a coward. I had thought about asking Dr. Minford back in Baltimore, but I chickened out. It was too heavy a burden to carry alone. If I couldn't share the knowledge with Jim, I didn't want it for myself. I was afraid that storing such a secret would taint my behavior toward Jim and throw me even more off-balance. But I did not want sole responsibility for planning Jim's funeral.

"Help me," I said.

I kneeled on the floor beside Jim as he offered just one word: "Catalina."

Neither of us belonged to a church although we both believed in God in a vague, unquestioning sort of way. Technically, we were Protestants. Jim had attended church as a child. I hadn't. The only call either of us had had for a minister in years was when we married and the fellow we came up with reflected our casual ties to the church. He was a home-improvement contractor who'd gotten a mail-order degree and quoted extensively during the ceremony from Kahlil Gibran and an Apache love prayer. He called us Helen and Tim throughout the service.

When Jim uttered "Catalina" I knew what he meant: a spiritual home where we had found joy amid despair, the place where his heart had last felt whole.

Jim told me he wanted to be cremated and his ashes returned to Catalina. The rest was up to me.

*   *   *   *   *   *   *   *

In those last weeks, Jim's body actively began dying and I spent more and more of my time tending to him. His right leg ballooned to twice its size with edema and the bed sores multiplied like some awful acne across his tailbone, back and bottom. He had dropped nearly half his body weight and a few of the tumors had become so pronounced we worried they would break through the skin. The one under his left armpit was the size of my fist.

When I was little I used to stand on my dad's feet while he danced me around the living room. After Jim was quite weak, and he needed to use the bathroom, that's how we would get there. He would stand on my feet and lay his arms across my shoulders while I held onto his waist. Then we'd shuffle to the bathroom, two dancers in a hopelessly choreographed ballet. The "bowel program," as the nurses called it, had become a challenge.

The only time Jim could seem to defecate was while he sat on a shower chair in the bathtub with water streaming down his back in hot ribbons. I'd kneel on the floor and hold him steady, then clean up after him.

As I held him, I would turn my head away, trying to create a curtain of privacy between us. Gradually, I would feel his body relax.

"You OK?" I'd ask. "Comfortable?"

"I'm all right. You?"

It was the same short exchange every time. Then we'd wait. After a while, that system just didn't work anymore. For a time, we kept a commode by the bed until one day I went to the pharmacy to buy adult diapers.

In those last weeks, I never left the bedroom without saying, "I love you." If Jim was to die when I was out of the room, I wanted him to have just heard those words.

Jim began using oxygen May 12. Just moving in bed could wear him out. But his failing body contained a functioning mind: He continued to talk on the telephone, watch TV and engage the nurse and me in conversation. In those final days, he fixated on the yellow alarm clock and the TV remote controller—I think because they represented order and control, elements that had disappeared from his own life.

On May 19, I walked into Darla Romano's office on Balboa Street. She was the social worker the hospice had assigned. "You need a hug," she said before I even had a chance to sit down. Then, to my amazement, she just stood there and held me.

At first, her warmth seemed like a slap, but after a few seconds, I began to relax. I wanted to collapse in Darla's strong arms. A tall woman with a warm, easy manner, Darla was the first person in all those months I really leveled with. I knew that what I had to say couldn't hurt her.

"Although Jim and Ellen are honestly sharing their feelings and thoughts about the disease process with each other, they tend to play the role of protector with family and friends," Darla wrote in her client log after that first session. She gave me her notes from our first therapy sessions shortly after Jim died. "It's hard for them to share their pain and imminent loss with others who expect them to be 'strong.' This keeps each of them more distant from their own sadness."

While I was with Darla, Jim was eating half of a cherry popsicle and a quarter-cup of JELL-O. It was as hearty a meal as he was to eat until he died ten days later. He was beginning to lose feeling in his limbs and he'd begun to sleep a lot. On May 25, Jim looked at me as if I was a riddle to solve. He didn't know who I was.

In his last days, I spoon-fed him. When he could no longer tolerate food, I rinsed his mouth with lemon glycerin swabs and ice chips and rubbed Vaseline into his dry, cracked lips. A yellow yeast had begun to grow in the fleshy parts of his mouth. Even then, when I walked through the bedroom door, Jim would smack the air with his lips, giving me a goldfish kiss.

"It's time to call Jim's family," the home nurse, Laurie Umeh, said after I told her Jim hadn't recognized me. "He won't last out the week. He's got three, maybe four days left."

Laurie, a quiet woman, had been checking in on us every other day since Jim had been released from the hospital. I knew she had a teenage son and was a single parent and that she cared mostly for AIDS patients. She hugged me and then left to arrange for full-time nursing care.

I walked upstairs to check on Jim. He hadn't spoken in twenty-four hours, his voice silenced by the disease. His face was blank, all expression erased from it. He looked as if he were under a spell. More than anything, I longed to hear the soothing tones of his voice. "Everything is going to be fine, Ellen," he would have told me. "I love you, Ellen," he would have said.

A couple of weeks earlier, Jim mentioned that he had begun to record some personal feelings on the tape recorder I'd given him for his birthday. Feeling like a thief, I scooped the recorder off the old oak night stand, ran downstairs and pressed PLAY.

"I had intended to have most of this tape deal with my feelings, our feelings, but mostly mine, on the business of life and death and how you deal with them when they hit you so hard in the face," I heard Jim say.

"But I'm finding that probably there's not that much of a need to do it. I mean what can you say? The biggest problem I'm going through, and I'm doing it right now, is the preliminaries, the stuff that leads up to death.

"I think it's easier for me right now than it is for

anybody else. People are worried about me and they're very sad I'm in this moribund condition but I think deep down, subconsciously, their real feelings are about themselves. They're thinking: What am I going to do? I'm going to be really sad when he dies. What will I look like at the funeral? Will I cry?

"I don't mean to say that in a bad way because I think the same thing about everybody that I'm close to. I've always hoped I would die before they would. I remember Ellen coming out of the bathroom one night just before she went to bed. This was before I had cancer. She came out of the bedroom and said, 'I really hope that I die before you do because I'd be so sad to be here without you'.

"That's the prevailing feeling and I think people who are in a moribund state feel the same way. They're glad if it's got to be somebody, it should be them and not the other person." Then Jim laughed. "Of course, better that it should be nobody at all."

I listened a while longer, seeking some sort of reassurance in the sound of his voice. A little later, I climbed up to our bedroom, peeled off my clothes and slipped my body beside Jim's. An empty silence filled the room as I waited for sleep, hoping for quick passage into the thick comfort of a dream.

CHAPTER
3

HIS LAST DAY

I always think of the day Jim died as the great divide in my life, harshly measuring everything into The Before and The After.

Talking about his illness on the tape-recording, Jim said he believed that some people look for a "certainty" in death that it just doesn't have. Now, looking back across that divide, I think I know what he means.

There are people who—watching you die or watching you mourn—desperately want some sort of guarantee that you're OK and, that in your place, they'd be OK too.

On the spring afternoon that he died, I was sitting at the dining-room table when I heard Jim's parents call me to his bedside. An almost ghostly presence on turquoise sheets, he looked hollow and wax-yellow in color, more mannequin than man. His mouth was slightly open, a noiseless zero. He looked liked he had been stunned into silence just as he was about to say something. Except for a few words, Jim hadn't spoken in four days.

There was a sense of expectancy in the room. It reminded me of that still, silent time right before it snows. Jim's father was standing at the foot of the bed, rubbing his son's cold feet with tired, calloused hands. As Jim's circulation system shut down, the chill in his feet crawled up his calves and over his knees, the warmth oozing out of him like toothpaste from a tube.

Gloria, Jim and I formed a circle around the bed,

where, a few hours earlier, Gloria had filled the stale air with lullabies. "Little man you're crying and I know why you're blue," she sang softly. "Someone took your kiddie car away." As a young child, the song had been "Jimmy's" favorite. In those last hours, it seemed the two ends of Jim's life—its start and finish—had converged into this single lullaby.

As the three of us gathered around the bed, I repeated the two words I had whispered to Jim all through the previous night: "Let go."

Jim's parents and his daughters, Aimée and Anne, had arrived two days earlier and his brother, Jeff, had flown in the evening before from New York. We had told Jim that Jeff was coming and he seemed to recognize him when he got there. Each of us had said goodbye.

"We're here, Jim. You're not alone." My voice sounded like it was coming from out of a tunnel. "Your mom and dad are here in the room. The girls have gone out for a few hours. We love you, Jim."

"It's OK to let go. We're all going to be fine. Relax, Jim, let go."

The home nurse, Agnes Lamb, had told us that although Jim could no longer see or speak, he probably could still hear. Suddenly, as we were standing there, Jim's parents, who are Baptists, began singing hymns, ventilating the room with Hosannas. Their voices startled me. Agnes, who had been sitting quietly in a corner, joined them. I had almost forgotten she was there.

"Turn your eyes upon Jesus," their strong voices urged. As they went on, they seemed to get louder.

"Look full in His wonderful face. And the things of the earth will grow strangely dim in the light of His glory and grace."

As I listened, a part of me felt left out because I didn't know the words. Still, I hoped Jim couldn't hear them. I don't believe he would have found Jesus songs particularly reassuring.

I didn't know Jim was dead until Agnes walked over and closed his eyes. An older woman, calm and efficient, Agnes took care of Jim during the four days before he died. Every morning, she'd show up for her eight-hour shift in a starched white uniform, white hose and white shoes with crepe soles. Her daughter had cancer, too. I don't know how she could look at Jim and not see her own child's face. After closing Jim's eyes, Agnes crossed his arms on his thin, bare chest and pulled the sheet up to his neck.

I couldn't stop staring at Jim's face. There seemed to be a hint of a smile on his lips, as if something had secretly pleased him. Watching him, I didn't want to forget anything—the breeze sneaking in through the sliding glass door, rattling the pink PLEASE DISTURB sign Jim had hung on the doorknob; the look of his skin against mine; the urge I had to shake him awake. More than anything, I didn't want the moment to dissolve into a cold collection of facts. At the foot of the bed, Jim's father finally released his son's feet and he and Gloria held one another in as sweet and intimate an embrace as I've seen. Then they held me.

"It's over now," Jim's dad said. "There's no more pain. Jimmy's gone."

I had been preparing for this moment for six months, but I didn't know what to feel or how to feel it. The dying had been so dramatic, so life-filled really, that the physical death was in some ways anti-climactic.

"This is it?" I thought to myself. "That's Jim and he's dead? That's his body and it's dead?"

I looked at Jim with morbid curiosity, somehow expecting him to move or open his eyes. I hugged his body, but I couldn't find *him* anywhere in that final embrace.

I felt emptied, stripped like a tree that has lost all its leaves. Jim had been right: There was no "certainty" here. My thickly forested life had turned into something yellowed, withered and coarse—a flat, featureless plain that disappeared into an endless horizon. This place wasn't even on the map.

I keep remembering Jim's eyes—like a deer's caught in a headlight. In those moments before he died, he seemed focused on a singular object no one else could see. I hope he wasn't frightened.

As Jim gave up his last breath, the digital clock by the bed snapped into a new minute: 4:25 p.m. It was May 29, 1987, a Friday. Jim would have been amused that the anniversary of his death frequently falls over Memorial Day weekend.

I believe Jim chose the moment he died—that he held on so that Jeff could say goodbye, and that he purposefully let go of his life at a time when his daughters were out of the house. Aimée had walked to a jewelry store to buy a locket for a snip of her father's hair she had been carrying in her wallet since Jim had first gone bald in January. Jeff and Anne, who had turned sixteen two days earlier, were together at "Jim's Tower." I had told them the tower meant something special to Jim and me.

Shortly after 4:30, standing at the tower, Anne told me she felt a "hard wind" and she remembers getting "literally a pain" in her heart. Turning to Jeff, she said, "We can go back now. He's dead."

Anne and Jeff got home first. Anne, though three years younger than her sister, was somehow sturdier during those few crazy days, perhaps because she was more accepting. The day after Jim collapsed in Baltimore, I had picked up Anne and driven her to the hospital. She told me then she believed Jim was dying and I don't think she ever was convinced otherwise.

While the rest of the family comforted one another, I watched the front door, afraid for the time when Aimée would walk through it. Nineteen-year-old Aimée, the daughter Jim once called his "soul." I shall never forget Aimée's shrill, piercing screams when I told her Jim was dead or the raw, inconsolable look of longing on her face.

As for me, I don't think I really began to feel the wretched bleakness of Jim's absence until several days after he died. His death created between us a chasm so deep, a space so vast, that at first I could not appreciate its measurements.

I do know that right after he died, I didn't want to leave the bedroom. As long as I could see him, he wasn't really lost to me. In those first moments, as I sat holding his lifeless hand, I heard Agnes call Jim's doctor and the crematorium from the telephone in the next room. When I heard her give the crematorium our address, I wanted to throw up.

"They'll be here for Jim's body in an hour," Agnes told me. "Jim's body," she had said. To me, he was still Jim. I would have to learn a new vocabulary.

I released his hand and stood, steeling myself.

"I need you to collect all of Jim's medications and put them by the bathroom sink."

Reluctantly, I walked downstairs, grabbed the

morphine syringes from the refrigerator and placed them in the bathroom next to a row of brown, plastic pill bottles. There were sleeping pills, pain pills, anti-nausea pills, anti-inflammatory pills. Head nurse Laurie Umeh, who had arrived by then, removed the syringes from their shiny, foil wrapping and shot the morphine into the toilet. Then she dumped the pills. After a half-dozen or so flushes, everything was gone, a swirling stew of Feel-Good washed into San Francisco's sewers. At that point, it wasn't Jim's death that was killing me, but a hundred other little things, like the sound of that toilet flushing.

Agnes and Laurie went home after that, and Jeff took Gloria and the girls for a drive while my father-in-law and I waited for the men from the crematorium. Three days earlier, I had driven to the Neptune Society offices near Tower Records down by Fisherman's Wharf, paid $569 and talked to a "counselor" about final arrangements.

Guiding me past a tall, glass case of urns, some of them ornate and costly, the woman proudly described the detail and workmanship of the various "models" available for my "loved one's" ashes. I felt like I was on a museum tour with a demented docent. I opted for a plain cardboard box, signed the paperwork ("in triplicate, please") and bolted.

As Jim's father and I waited for the men from the Neptune Society to arrive, I prayed for only one thing—that they complete their "home removal" (their words, not mine) before Aimée and Anne returned. I didn't even want to think about them bumping into the girls on the stairs with Jim's body.

Again, I watched my front door, dreading the time

when I would have to open it. I heard the man's heavy footsteps on the stairs even before he rang the bell.

I half-opened the door.

"Where's your partner?" I asked.

The man was disheveled—sweating and breathing heavily, almost panting. He was wearing brown polyester trousers that were a couple of inches too long, and the bottoms were folded into a permanent crease in the spot where his heels kept catching the frayed ends.

"I'm by myself," he said. "I'll manage."

But how? There were four flights of stairs, plus the steps up to the bedroom. I walked upstairs while the man trailed behind me with a stretcher. I didn't offer to help.

Jim's father and I huddled in a corner by the dresser and watched as the fellow laid the stretcher on the rust colored carpet beside the bed. Jim had been dead for an hour, but I felt he needed me there to protect him.

The man, still sweating, scooped Jim's body off the bed as if he were a sack of potatoes and began to wrap him in plastic—similar to the thick wrapping that's used to winterize leaky windows. I hadn't expected the plastic.

"Please," I said. "Be gentle. Don't hurt him." The man looked at me as if I were crazy, and continued to unroll the plastic from what looked like a giant spool of Saran Wrap.

"Don't worry, lady," he said. "He can't feel anything." I pushed the man away as he started to wrap Jim's face in the clear plastic.

"He won't be able to breathe. You'll suffocate him," I said, realizing my mistake before the words were out.

I felt disoriented, caught in unfamiliar territory between the taken-for-granted past and the unbelievable present.

"And I want that sheet," I demanded. Our turquoise top sheet was folded in the plastic wrapping.

"Most people don't want the sheets," the man said.

"I want it."

He loosened the sheet, tossed it on the bed and then tightened the plastic wrap around Jim. Even through the thick plastic, I could see the frozen expression on Jim's face.

With no ceremony at all, the man silently loaded him onto the gurney, covered him with a brown blanket and strapped him onto the narrow stretcher. Then, gripping the top of the stretcher, the man pushed it out of the bedroom as he would a wheelbarrow and began to slide it down the stairs, one step at a time. Every time he stopped, I saw Jim's head bounce.

"Take it easy," Jim's father yelled. He ran in front of me, picked up the bottom end of the gurney and, together, the two men carried it down to the street.

As I waited upstairs, they slid the stretcher into the back of a dirty van. The man slammed the door shut, started up the van and drove away. He was probably already thinking about what he was going to eat for dinner and whether he'd make it home in time to catch "Wheel of Fortune." When Jim's father came back into the apartment, he found me sitting on the top step outside our bedroom.

"I can't believe that jerk. Are you OK?" I asked.

Jim's dad sank hopelessly onto a step next to me. "I should never have let him touch Jimmy," he said. "I should have said something."

For several minutes, we just sat.

"It doesn't seem possible he's not coming back," I said. "If it's OK, I'm going into the bedroom. I'll be out in a little while."

seventeen days earlier so that she could be with Jim and me while he was dying. She had already found an apartment and was working in the personnel department of a computer magazine publishing firm. Just like that, she decided to move. It must run in the family.

Anybody looking at us through the window that night would have witnessed an ordinary family sharing dinner over candlelight. That's what struck me—how ordinary we all were. I was humbled by the thought that this had happened to so many other people—that this ache that was gnawing through each of us at the table had claimed so many other families, not just this one. The knowledge didn't soothe as much as awe me.

Up until then, I had known only two family members to die—my grandfather when I was thirteen and an uncle when I was sixteen. Those deaths, though, were facts in my family history, not a piece of the air I breathed.

Over dinner, Jim and Gloria put their own pain away and tried to comfort the rest of us. "He's at peace now," my father-in-law said, his kind eyes taking us all in. "He's not in pain. I feel sure he's watching us all now, and he'd want us to be OK."

Maybe all those things were true—I had even said a couple of them to myself—but the words were as empty as the bed upstairs. I was beginning to understand that this was going to be a lonely, private struggle.

I kept thinking of all the "lasts:" The last time I had eaten by candlelight was Jim's birthday. The last time I had sat at the dining-room table was when Jim and Gloria had called me up to the bedroom that afternoon. The last time I had brushed my teeth, Jim had been alive—crazy stuff like that. And I kept glancing at my watch, measuring the time since Jim had died.

There had been such a timelessness, a seamles[s] to the days that Jim lived in the apartment wit[h] Even after his body was hauled off, I had to wall[?] into the bedroom and look at the bed to convince [me] he wasn't still there.

In that last month, I had lived in a state of suspe[nse] a kind of floating almost, but trudging back int[o] room I began to feel more a part of the earth tha[n] air. I felt like I was wearing ankle weights. Each ste[p] so heavy. I knelt on the floor beside the bed and [put] my face on Jim's pillow, imagining his head in the [place] of it instead of my own. Even with the glass door cr[acked] open, I could still smell sickness in the musty [air. I] stripped the sheets and sat on a corner of the bar[e bed,] hoping I'd feel something of Jim in the room. Bu[t all I] felt was an emptiness.

A week later I received a letter from the exec[utive] director of the local Neptune Society, apologizin[g for] the breakdown in the system on the day Jim die[d. In] San Francisco, because so many houses have steps[,] people are routinely assigned to home removals.

"I am truly sorry that you experienced this uncall[ed] performance. I can assure you that I will take steps nece[ssary] to prevent this from happening to other families,[" the] director said in response to a letter I had written. "..[I] thank you for bringing this incident to my attenti[on. I] realize even for you to do so reopens a wound."

Reopens a wound? It hadn't had a chance to c[lose,] and on that day I wondered if it ever would.

The night Jim died, Gloria made spaghetti and s[alad] and we all crowded around the dining-room tab[le:] Aimée and Anne, Jim and Gloria, Jeff and my s[ister] Barbie, who had moved from Baltimore to San Fran[cisco]

The doorbell rang in the middle of dinner and Jim and Gloria sprang up to answer it. They had been expecting Jon, their second-oldest child, to arrive at some point. We knew he'd had car trouble. A mailman, he and his wife, Roxie, had driven in from New Mexico.

"You're too late," Gloria said. "He's already gone."

"I'm glad," Jon told her.

I had never met Jon and when he rounded the corner into the dining room, my jaw fell. He looks so much like Jim; his face, his walk, even the way he loosely folds himself into a chair when he sits. I can remember wanting to touch him.

It's strange meeting your brother-in-law for the first time when the person you have in common has just been carried dead out of the house. But then, the first time I had met Jim and Gloria was in the receiving line at my wedding. At the time, they weren't thrilled about our marriage, and we weren't even sure they would show up.

"Hi, I'm Ellen," I said, pasting on a smile and moving toward Jon. I didn't feel like the Ellen I knew, so I did the next best thing: I imitated myself. I did a lot of that the first few months after Jim died. It was the only way I could seem to function.

After a while, Barbie drove back to her new apartment in Redwood City and everyone but Jim and Gloria returned to the motel. We had decided to hold a memorial service the following Saturday.

Once everyone left, Jim and Gloria disappeared into my office, where they had been sleeping on our trundle bed. I could hear the murmur of their voices behind the closed door. Jim had been the oldest of their four children, and I could only imagine their pain. I knew it was different than mine. I was glad they were there.

Even more than my own parents, I gravitated toward them because they were part Jim.

Glad, finally, for the privacy, I crawled into bed, caressing the empty side that was Jim's. The bed seemed awfully wide without him in it. Through the opening in the closet door, I could see his shirts and jeans hanging on the left side, his shoes and an old pair of scuffed black motorcycle boots lined up across the floor beneath them. It occurred to me I would have to do something with his clothes.

In a basket by the bed were the birthday and get-well and thinking-of-you cards that had arrived over the past month. "You know you're really sick when the thinking-of-you cards begin to outnumber the get-well ones," Jim had said to me one day after reading his mail.

I picked a couple of cards out of the basket. One of them, a Peanuts card featuring the Lucy character, was from me. "I'd climb the highest mountain. I'd swim the deepest sea. I'd cross the hottest desert," it said. "Just to let you be with me."

Just to let you be with me. That's all I had wanted, focused upon, for six months.

Also in the card basket was a college catalog that had shown up in the mailbox the previous week. In the last days, as Jim began to slide into unconsciousness, his father had read him pretty much the entire catalog, just so Jim could hear the sound of his voice.

A couple of times, I had walked into the room while my father-in-law was reciting the stilted language about English majors, financial aid and graduation requirements. From the tone of his voice, you would have thought he had just struck gold.

"How about that, Jimmy," he'd say. "I know you've

read most of these books required for that English major. Remember when you won the school spelling bee in the fifth grade and never said anything to us about it? Your teacher finally told us. Or, in the eighth grade, when you wrote that essay on 'The Life of a Nickel,' I remember Gloria telling you then you should be a writer. We're proud of you, Jimmy."

He had stationed himself on a chair beside the head of the bed for the better part of two days, reading that catalog, telling Jim how proud he had made him, and polishing dusty old memories as if they were precious gems. Maybe he *had* struck gold.

Looking around the room, I saw badges of Jim's illness all around me: the walker, an oxygen tank, the bandages for his bed sores, the walkie-talkies from Radio Shack we had used when we were on separate floors of the apartment, the yellow pan he had kept by the bed to throw up in.

I couldn't stop thinking about the chiseled thinness of Jim's face, which had so frightened Aimée and Anne. Would I ever be able to picture him well again? Would any of us? I had tried to prepare the girls when I picked them up at the airport, but what can you say: Your father doesn't look like your father anymore? No words could have prepared them for his face. It was beyond their imagining.

"It smells in here," Aimée had said as she was climbing the last few stairs to the top floor of the apartment when we first got home. She was right. Jim's bed sores had started to stink.

Aimée never made it into the bedroom. She buckled over and pulled back just before she got to the door.

"That's not him in there," she said, the panic rising

in her voice, washing over her like a high tide. "I'm not going in. I can't."

After talking to Darla, the social worker who had stopped by to check in on us, Aimée changed her mind. At Darla's suggestion, Aimée sat on a director's chair by the bed with a photograph of Jim in her lap. It was a picture my father had taken of Jim and me at the emerald bay in Catalina. She couldn't bear to look at Jim, so she talked to the man in the five-by-seven photograph instead.

"I love you, Dad," she said, her head hanging over the picture. Her hands trembled as she held the photograph.

"I care so much about you. And, Dad, I wouldn't mind if you left. Can you hear me, Dad? Can you hear me?"

Although Anne had told me Jim looked like a "monster," she had wandered in and out of the room a lot those last two days. "Today is my 16th birthday and it sucks," she had written in her journal the night the girls had arrived in San Francisco. "My dad only has a few days left to live. Aimée and I flew out to be with him. It was a terrible experience. He can no longer see or speak."

On the day before he died: "Dad is not doing well. I have been spending a lot of time with him. There's not much time left now."

As I lay in bed after dinner, Anne was in her motel room writing this entry: "Dad died today. Even though I wasn't in the house, I knew when he had died. He is at peace now. I miss my dad tonight."

I missed him, too, but I didn't want to miss him too much—not then. I was afraid that if I allowed myself to miss Jim, the force of the loss would flatten me. It wouldn't be some sort of warm, fuzzy "letting go," more like diving into a drained swimming pool. Contact of that kind would be merciless.

I wanted to call my parents, but I decided I had delivered enough anguish for one day.

"He's gone," I had whispered into the telephone to my mother earlier.

I couldn't bring myself to say "dead."

My father had wanted to drive up immediately, but I'd told him I would fly to Los Angeles to visit them for a few days instead. Thinking of Aimée and Anne, I was guilty I even had a father.

Before turning off the light, I plugged in the neon sculpture of a palm tree and sunset that I had surprised Jim with in early May. I had intended to give him the sculpture as an anniversary present, but like Father's Day, our wedding anniversary is in June. So I'd given it to him early.

As the neon wrapped the room in warm strips of pink, yellow and green light, I wondered where Jim was and what really happens after you die. Was he watching me now? I wondered if he'd send me some sort of message and I prayed he would visit my dreams. Then, sliding my body over to his side of the bed, I practiced saying, "My husband is dead. My husband is dead. My husband is dead."

CHAPTER
4

WIDOW'S WALK

Waking up the morning after he died, my hand strayed involuntarily across the sheets toward Jim. Somehow, I had forgotten he wasn't there.

It was late, almost 9:00.

As if to clear up any confusion as to his whereabouts, I heard my mother-in-law's confident voice announce from the next room, "Jimmy's with the Lord."

"Yes, at 4:25 yesterday," she was saying into the telephone. Gloria sounded almost happy. "He was ready to go."

"Were you really, Jim?" I thought as I rolled out of bed. "What have you done with yourself? What happens now?"

Busy work is what happens.

Gloria and I were on the telephone for most of the day notifying friends and relatives. By the third or fourth call, I was proficient at it. I could almost say the words "Jim died" and not feel their sharp edge.

"Hi, this is Ellen."

I had called a friend, Charlie Stott, and his answering machine had commanded me to speak after the beep.

"Jim died yesterday."

Had his kitchen door been open, Charlie might have heard me leave the message. At the time, he was in his back yard in Virginia inspecting the season's first blossoms on his cherry trees.

"The memorial service will be Saturday. Come if you can.

After hanging up, I kept imagining Charlie listening to his messages and learning from a disembodied voice that a person he had thought of as alive was, in fact, dead. I envied the people I called. As far as they were concerned, Jim was a living, breathing human being until the second I told them otherwise. It seemed an awesome power to me. With the sound of my voice, I could make a person disappear.

Every time I repeated the news, a part of my own history died. I could almost feel myself growing smaller. *Ellen and Jim to Ellen. We to I. Us to me. Ours to mine.* Already, I was beginning to readjust my space.

Walking through that first day without Jim, I felt otherworldly, as if I were floating in blankness. Thinking about the empty days stacked in front of me, I hoped not for happiness, but for relief.

"I'll see you back here in a few days," I told Aimée and Anne as they boarded a flight to Baltimore the day after Jim died. The girls looked washed-out, stunned, the animation erased from their faces. Aimée was dressed in the plaid shirt and rolled-up blue sweat pants she had pulled out of Jim's closet, where she had gone early that morning in search of something that smelled of him.

My whole concept of airports changed as we waited for their plane that day. Instead of paying attention to the warm reunions that occur as eager passengers meet their loved ones, I began looking for the sad people. They are there, you know—the solitary women reading books about broken relationships as they hug their styrofoam coffee cups; men who cannot mask their tears; children who don't even try.

I was on an airplane myself the next day—to Los Angeles.

"Honey, we're so sorry."

Mother and Dad, waiting for me at the gate at LAX, threw themselves around my body like a warm blanket and began rubbing my back and shoulders, as if they were trying to resuscitate me.

We had barely cleared the front door before I began inspecting their house for evidence of Jim. Perhaps he had left something behind from our visit in March. Maybe I'd sense him in the guest room or by the swimming pool. I was open to all possibilities. But Jim wasn't anywhere there. The rest of the day, I sat with my legs tucked under me on the couch, trying not to think.

"Let's get your hair cut for the memorial service," Mother said at one point. "It needs it, honey. I know Pierre will fit you in."

The suggestion felt like a slap.

"A hair cut?"

How could anyone be thinking about something as banal as a haircut when a husband has just died? I realized later I didn't want to change the way I had appeared when Jim had last seen me.

I had looked to Mother for comfort, but she was in so much pain herself, she was unable to provide it. Mother is undone by death, and Jim's was no different. She was unraveled, at loose ends. At the time, she simply couldn't talk about it, at least not to me. I have never felt more distant from her.

In an attempt to boost my spirits, and probably her own as well, Mother took me shopping. She must have spent hundreds on clothes for me that afternoon. It wasn't until we got home that I noticed everything I had selected was khaki green or tan. Numb colors, as I thought of them later.

After shopping, we stopped for lunch at a restaurant where the tables are covered with white paper. Mother, sitting across from me, took a red crayon from a can on the tabletop and began writing.

Even upside down, I could make out the words: "We miss you, Jim."

It was the best she could do.

Jim used to say that if you don't expect too much from people, they won't disappoint you. During the years we were together, I had come to believe completely in Jim and in the sturdy net of our relationship. I had not expected that to change. Looking back now, I sometimes think I skipped over the "Why me?" stage but, on some level, I will always wonder "Why him?"

                    *   *   *   *   *   *   *   *

Back in San Francisco a couple of days later, I picked up Anne at the airport. She had decided to return to California earlier than Aimée. Like me, Anne felt drawn to the place Jim had died. The apartment on Grandview provided more than a roof and a view. It was the place I felt most whole. It housed the sum of my parts and for many, many weeks, I ached every time I left it.

The night she arrived, Anne crawled into bed next to me.

"You won't be scared?" I worried that sleeping in the bed where her father had died would frighten her.

"I need to do this," she said. "I want to do this. But let's keep the light on."

Anne claimed my side of the bed, and I moved over

to Jim's. Together we lay there, looking blankly at the ceiling, searching for answers where there were none.

"I dreamt about him on the plane on the way back to Baltimore," Anne said after a long silence. "I could hear somebody singing in my head. Then I got to the airport and he was there, dressed all in white. I told him, 'I want to come with you, Dad. Take me with you.' He told me I couldn't."

A few minutes later, she asked: "Do you think he sees us? Can you feel him?"

"I do, Anne, I really do."

As I fell asleep, I thought how lucky she was to have seen Jim again, if only in a dream.

To me, Anne is part-daughter, part-sister, part-friend. There are fifteen years between us. Up until the night she slept in our bed, I had always thought of her as "Jim's daughter." It was only through him that we were connected. That began to change after he died. I like to think of it as one of the gifts Jim left us.

*   *   *   *   *   *   *   *

Planning a memorial service is a lot like throwing a party, with the usual considerations: Will the people who don't know one another mingle? Does the house look OK? And, if not exactly a rollicking good time, will you be able to create an event that folks will, at the least, find meaningful?

One of the best parties I have attended was Jim's memorial service. So many folks who cared about him all in one place—nothing could have filled me up as much as that did. It helped plug the odd lonesomeness that had begun to seep through the underside of my skin.

Most of the fifty-some people who crowded into the apartment had witnessed our marriage two years earlier. The young ring-bearer was there, our best man, the maid of honor, our parents—the ironic offerings of a mysterious timekeeper.

"Boy, did he have love," my father-in-law announced during the service after playing excerpts from the tape Jim had made three weeks before. "He loved people. That was his favorite thing—people. He understood them. And afraid? You heard him. He wasn't afraid. He felt sorry for us. Can you imagine?"

I hungered for Jim, and each time someone offered a memory of him, I felt a little less empty. At times, it was as if he were absent and not dead at all. But just as I would turn around to search the room for his face, or open my mouth to call his name, I would remember.

During the service, my cousin, Pamela, pulled me aside. After learning Jim had died, she said she had reluctantly broken the news to Derrick, her six-year-old son. Derrick, the ring-bearer at our wedding, had been including Jim in his prayers for months. When she went into Derrick's bedroom a few hours later to kiss him goodnight, Pamela heard her son say: "God, please let Jim into Heaven and make him feel better and please make a medicine so he doesn't get sick anymore. Please also have him say hi to Abraham Lincoln."

Another friend gave me a homemade card she had found tucked in her seven-year-old daughter's school bag: "Sweet young men should not smoke!!," Amanda had written across the green graph paper, which she had colored with rainbows, a heart and flowers. "You are sweet. You are young and we all love you very very very very much. But if your life is going to end, we all will still remember you evry (sic) year and weekend. Love is no smoking!!(sic)." No one had asked Amanda to write the card.

For many months, I sought stories of Jim to add to my private reserves and I read and re-read the condolence cards, hoping to recapture a piece of him. The well-thumbed cards, dozens of them, now crowd a box next to the cards that wished us wedding congratulations. The last time I looked through them the dry red rubber bands they were wrapped in disintegrated in my hand.

The wedding and the memorial service—I twin them in my mind, just like the cards in that box. It's an odd symmetry—one short marriage framed between those two events.

Greeting people at the memorial service, I was held, stroked, and kissed and I began to feel almost weightless.

"You're so young," several folks offered that day. One woman even assured me: "Pretty, smart girl like you, you'll find someone else. You have a long life ahead of you."

After the memorial service, everyone walked out to the rooftop deck, where each of us released a helium balloon. A few minutes later, the afternoon sky was crowded with colorful balloons, messages to Jim.

"Goodbye, Jim," the voices began to say around me. "Goodbye." Such a simple word. It stuck in my throat. One of the hardest things I've ever had to do was let go of my balloon.

A few months later, I dreamt about Jim for the first time. It was our wedding day and as we walked hand in hand among well-wishers, Jim began to float away. I grabbed his hand in both of mine and tried to pull him down. At first, I laughed. It seemed funny—until I could no longer hold onto him. There was nothing I could do but let go.

*   *   *   *   *   *   *   *

Two days after the memorial service the last of the visitors were saying goodbye again—this time to me.

Jim and Gloria were flying home to San Antonio. Anne was going with them. It was June 8, my second wedding anniversary.

Gloria and Anne stood on the sidewalk in front of the Southwest Airlines gate while Jim lugged their bags out of the trunk of the Nova. Then he came over and hugged me hard.

"Happy anniversary," he said as I got ready to leave. The words bounced off his lips like bubbles. "Jimmy was a mighty lucky man." Others had remembered our anniversary, but he was the only person to openly acknowledge it, in celebration instead of sadness. But that's Jim's dad.

From the airport, I drove directly to the Neptune Society offices to pick up Jim's ashes. Wedding and memorial service, congratulations and condolences, anniversary and ashes. Everything was so mixed up.

"You called yesterday," I announced to the receptionist, trying to find a steady voice to speak in. "I'm here to pick up the ashes of James E. Thomas III."

I paused. "My husband."

"Of course, Mrs. Thomas."

My name wasn't Thomas, but hearing her call me that soothed me—I guess because I kept having to remind myself who I was.

The receptionist handed over a sack with a gold cardboard box in it. The box was heavy, six or seven pounds. I had thought ashes would be light, almost weightless, like sawdust or peanut shells.

At home, I placed the box on the dining room table. I stared at it but I couldn't bring myself to open it.

I cracked open a beer and tapped a corner of the box with it.

"Hello, Jim, you in there?"

Finally, I removed the cover. Dipping my hand inside, I ran my fingers through the tan, granular remains, which reminded me of kitty litter and not of ashes at all. I sniffed the edges of the box—no smell. Jim was not in the box. I replaced the lid, finished my beer and walked upstairs to the office, where I thought I might find him.

To commemorate our wedding anniversary, I pulled out all the letters and cards Jim had written to me. There were dozens of them, a chain leading back to June 3, 1983, the first night we spent together.

At *The Morning Herald* in Hagerstown, Jim had been in charge of the reporters' daybook, a directory of daily news events and story assignments. When I got to work that June afternoon, mine had said: "File final prison story. File story on lawyer who's being sued for fraud. Check early cops, please. *And then meet us at the Antietam Tavern after work....*" In the end, that single line in the daybook had delivered us to one another.

Jim liked to design Top Ten lists, and among the letters I had strewn across the office carpet was his listing of the ten reasons he had wanted to marry me.

"1. I couldn't help it. It seemed like such a natural thing to do, despite the difficult and unusual circumstances we were in.

"2. I didn't want to lose you, and though I know marriage is no guarantee that two people won't drift apart, it at least improves the odds that they will do their best to grow close and stay together. I wanted to improve my chances with you.

"3. You intrigue me, totally. The more I know about you— what you have done, what you think, who you were and who you are—the more I want to know. Thus, my questions and quizzes and conversations. I never want to stop getting to know you."

I consumed each word, breathing Jim in, until I got to No. 10.

"There's nothing I would rather have done with my life."

*   *   *   *   *   *   *   *

I flew to Los Angeles that night with Jim's ashes packed inside a red gym bag. I don't know whether it was because the bag was so heavy or because I was clutching it so tightly, but as I ran to catch my plane, the canvas hand strap cut a groove in my clenched palm.

When the airport shuttle driver deposited me at my parents' house, my father scooped the bag out of my hand. I never touched it or the gold box again. Boarding the ferry for Catalina the following afternoon, it was Dad who carried the bag.

"I want to take him back to that emerald cove we visited in March, the one in the photographs," I told Mother and Dad. "Remember how happy he was that day?"

They nodded in numb agreement, and when we arrived in Avalon, Catalina's only town, we rented a golf cart—the primary mode of transportation on the tiny island. We decided to leave the motel at six the next morning so that we could spread Jim's ashes before the summer tourists had even had a chance to think about their first cup of coffee.

When I was a kid, my parents played a lot of Nat King Cole tapes on their old reel-to-reel recorder. There's a song I remember that was popularized by Nat King Cole, but it was Al Jolson, in the 1920s, who wrote the lyrics to *Avalon*:

I found my love in Avalon beside the Bay
I left my love in Avalon and sail'd away....

Just beyond the Moorish-style casino on Avalon Bay, at the end of a walkway shaded by palm trees, there is a small, quiet beach called Descanso. As it turned out, we weren't able to drive the golf cart to the emerald cove—it was only accessible by tour bus. So, on the gray, misty morning we scattered Jim's ashes, we piled into golf cart No. 54 and drove to Descanso Beach at Avalon Bay.

Dad jumped out of the white golf cart with the gym bag, while I blew up a beach ball imprinted with a crude blue and brown map of the world. The balloon I had released at the memorial service had carried the same design.

"I wanted to send Jim off with the world," I had told Mother earlier. "That's what he was to me. Somehow, I feel like we're giving him back."

We must have looked strange—the three of us. Two women, a man, a beach ball and red gym bag, positioned at the water's edge.

"OK, Dad. I'm ready."

My father removed his white canvas shoes, rolled up his trousers and lifted the box out of the bag. Behind me, I heard Mother intone, again and again: "The Lord is my shepherd. I shall not want. He maketh me to lie down in green pastures, He leadeth me beside the still waters...."

Dad walked into the water, past the smooth brown rocks I could see just below the surface. He stopped when his feet touched sand, maybe twenty feet from where I was standing. From the shoreline, I watched his hand disappear into the box, and then emerge with a handful of ash. He threw out his fist, spread his fingers, then paused as if poised to catch a fly ball. Then he repeated the motion. Each time he fanned his fingers, a sprinkling of Jim's ashes floated into the water like confetti caught in a downwind.

I threw the beach ball toward my father, and twisted my wedding ring around my finger, wondering whether to toss it, too, into the swirling, green waters. But I couldn't bring myself to do it.

Later, we learned that in Spanish *descansar* means *to rest*.

In earlier times, sailors' widows in seaport towns congregated along the "widow's walk," searching the flat horizon for the one thing that would always elude them. Like theirs, this narrow strip of beach would become a part of my interior landscape, and on that overcast morning, I understood what the women were looking for. The horizon marks the limit of vision, but it is where the imagination begins.

Walking the short shoreline of Descanso, I recalled the pale insides of Jim's elbows, his flat feet, the way he teased me when I took myself too seriously and challenged me when I grew lazy. Now, it seemed, there was nothing at the edge of things, no one around the corner to save me.

In the tape-recording, Jim had called me a "soldier,

fighting every step of the way" for him. At Descanso, one war ended, and another began.

Pondering the rickety logic of my new life, I wondered: With Jim gone, who would I bother with the hundred little questions that make up a day: "Will you mail this on your way out?" "Can you get that jar off the top shelf?" "Did you remember to turn off the coffee pot?" "What did I do with my keys?" "What time do you want to eat?"

Would anyone care that I forgot my umbrella and got drenched on the way to the grocery store or that I saved $4 with coupons when I got there?

Without Jim, who would verify the contents of my memory? Fill the gaps in stories I couldn't remember? Finish my sentences?

Who would scratch the places I couldn't reach?

Who would call just to inquire how my day was going and who would answer when I pushed open the front door, and yelled into the darkness: "Anybody home?"

It's the little things that fill up a life, the loose change, and standing on the Catalina shoreline, I reached into deep, empty pockets.

JIM: A FATHER, A SON

Nothing like serious illness and death forces us to examine the contents of our hearts. Grief lets us know who we really are.

When Jim died, Aimée and Anne lost a father. Gloria and Jim lost a son. "We've all been wounded," Anne told me once. "Dad's death hurt. His absence hurts. But we've each worked through it—in our own ways, in our own time. I guess the good thing about a scar is that it symbolizes a healing."

Here, in interviews five years after Jim's death, Jim's parents and daughters recount their loss.

ANNE

A month before Jim died, Anne picked up her address book, turned to "T" for Thomas and swatted across her father's name and address with a felt-tip pen until all that was left was a black smudge. Then she flipped forward a couple of pages, and under "U," Anne slowly began to write out my last name.

"That same day, I put his pictures in boxes, things he'd given me, letters," she told me during a visit to Lake Tahoe, the community in northern California where I lived at the time. "I wanted it over with. I had for all those months accepted the fact that he was dying, and I just wanted it over. I don't even know where the box is anymore. Now, I just have one thing that was his—that red sweater vest that he wore for years and years. That vest is the only thing I wanted after he died. It stirred physical memories. I remember going into the newsroom after school and he'd be wearing it. I keep it in my bottom drawer. Every now and then, I take it out of the drawer, look at it, smell it, touch it.

"I was just a sophomore in high school that December when Dad was diagnosed. I'd been having problems in school and I was just starting to turn around. He called, and I remember thinking: 'Oh God, here it goes again.' I was afraid my grades were going to go down.

"All those months, I knew he was going to die. There was never a question in my mind he was going to live. I'd sit at home and cry all the time. Deep down inside, I knew what was happening. I had dreamt a couple of times that he died. Six months before the brain tumor was diagnosed, I dreamt he was going to die from smoking. In every dream I have now about him, he's young and healthy—the ideal, young dad.

"When Dad moved, that really pissed me off. He should have spent those months with Aimée and me. There was no closure, and I've had to work through it in my dreams, in my subconscious, with my therapist. I wish we could have spent more time together. When I did see him that last time, it just blew me away. Maybe if it had been a gradual process, it wouldn't have been so bad. A friend told me, 'No matter what he looks like, remember he's still your father.' That's the only reason I could stand there and look at him. He was scary. He looked like a monster.

"I remember telling him mainly that Aimée was going to be OK. I don't know. She's always been someone to be concerned about. I told him I loved him. From that day on, it seems like everything fell apart: People kept telling me, 'You need to be there for Aimée. You need to be there for your mother.' I remember saying repeatedly, 'I'm just a kid. I'm young. I'm just a kid.'

"My way of dealing with it was not to fall apart about it. It's easier to comfort someone else. It avoided how I was feeling, but it helped Aimée cope. One time, I was trying to talk to Dad and she pushed me out of the way. I was so angry, but it wasn't supposed to be a time of anger. The best way to deal with the anger was to feel sorry for Dad.

"I still think about Dad a lot. There's an everyday awareness, but the incredibly heightened feelings are gone. The experience of his particular death generated a whole series of questions: Where do we go after we die? Is there anything after we die? Does it really matter?

"In those first months after he died, all I wanted to do was be with my friends and family. I got trashed that entire summer. I just couldn't explain what was going on to sixteen-year-old friends. They couldn't understand. They couldn't comfort me.

"There was so much pain. It was a time for total pain. I lashed out at my boyfriend. I lashed out at my mother. I dropped out of high school. I spent a whole year feeling sorry for myself. I felt empty, lonely. There was all this pain inside. For a good two years, I was angry. Then I just kind of snapped out of it. I took the GED, enrolled in college, stopped smoking, stopped drinking excessively and moved out on my own. I was only seventeen, but I felt I had to replant myself, somehow.

"After the pain, there came an acceptance. I feel peaceful now. What's upsetting is talking about how I once felt. I feel peaceful now. The experience of losing Dad and what came after have enlarged what I do while I'm here on this earth. *This* counts. *Here* counts. *Now* counts."

AIMÉE

Aimée, then a sophomore in college, had just walked out of a philosophy of religion class, when a girlfriend stopped her and told her to call her mother.

"I ran to the nearest pay phone and called Mom, and she said she was going to pick me up, that Dad had a brain tumor.

"I gasped. I couldn't breathe, and I was trying not to cry," Aimée told me as we talked on a bench at the Baltimore Zoo. "I figured that if I started crying, I wouldn't be able to stop.

"For the longest time, I didn't think he would die. I figured he could be fixed. Everything can be fixed. I remember wanting to be in complete control because I figured others wouldn't be. After I saw him that first day at the hospital, I went home and started drinking. I didn't stop drinking for a long time after that. It wasn't how much I drank, but when and why. I needed it to numb me, to make things fun. I drank for the next two years.

"I drank before I went to see Dad, and I drank while I was there with him. I felt somehow it would make things better. I regret it to this day. I was just so worried about him. Nothing really bad had happened to me or my father. I wanted it to be somebody else, anybody else, not him. He was my favorite. When I was little, I wanted to marry him when I grew up.

"One of my favorite memories goes back to when I was ten, and I pull it up sometimes when I'm sad. Dad was playing guitar at a hippie place, and he was warming up with the band—just acoustic stuff. I leaned over his shoulder and somebody said something about me being his girlfriend. I just smiled and smiled and smiled. I thought he was so special.

"One of my regrets is that I'd like to have him here now when I'm really getting together as a person. Back then, I wasn't doing anything. I was self-destructive. I'm afraid he was disappointed. I think he'd be proud of my accomplishments now.

"When he moved to California, I was relieved because everything would happen away from me, but I was angry he was leaving, too, so I reacted with my usual response: Fine, OK, so go ahead and give me another beer. The next thing I remember I was talking to him on the phone from California and his voice was really slurred because of the pain medication. Having your father be out of control like that is weird. Every time I talked to him he was less and less there. If he'd been shot or killed in a car accident, maybe it would have been different. He was so degraded by his illness. After one of those conversations, I threw furniture and slammed dishes against the wall. It hurt because I wanted him to have more than that.

"When I saw him in San Francisco, I knew he was dying. Not only was the acknowledgment there, but the wish that he would. Going through that metamorphosis must have been so painful. It was painful for me to see him suffer. I didn't want to go in the room that first day, but (the social worker) Darla had said, 'Do you think you might regret it if you don't?' I figured I'd already regretted a lot, so I went in. Looking at his face, I wanted to shoot him or kill him just to get rid of him. Let him go away! Get rid of him, and just let me get normal!

"When my grandmother died a few years ago, I thought, 'Oh, no, not again. You have to go through this thing all over again.' It's tedious, it's painful, and then it's over and you have to deal with the weirdness of somebody disappearing.

"Dad's death slapped me in the face about mortality and the fragility of life, and the taking-for-granted of things: people, situations, health. I think about things more deeply now, and I appreciate life and existence, not just my own but everything around me.

"When I got home after Dad's memorial service, I put pictures of him up all over the walls and doors, a shrine to Jim Thomas. Now, I just have one picture of him in my room. I wore his T-shirts, and I ate bologna with peanut butter sandwiches because that's what he used to eat. I wanted to extend the memories. I was afraid that eventually all memories of Jim Thomas would be lost.

"Sometimes, I let myself play with the idea that he's still alive. I'll think I see him walking down the street. If I see a man with Dad's characteristics, I watch him because I like to see those characteristics alive again. Sometimes, I'll see an old man hobbling down the sidewalk, and I'll think he'll turn around and have Dad's face, like the end of a mystery."

GLORIA

Under her bed in San Antonio, Gloria keeps three

cardboard boxes filled with mementos. "I have a box of Jimmy, a box of my mom and a box of my dad," she told me on a summer afternoon as we sat at her kitchen table. "The surprise is that Jimmy's there this soon.

"When people ask me how many children I have, I'm not always sure how to respond. Do I say four? Or do I say three? I never thought any of my children would go before me. It never entered my mind. I'd never known anyone to lose an adult child. You just expect your children to outlive you.

"I remember going to the church Christmas pageant a few weeks after Jimmy was diagnosed. A girl told me her brother had had a brain tumor and had just died. That's the first time I thought about his dying. I kept it inside. I was really kind of controlled. People would ask me how he was doing, and I was fine until I had to tell them. One day, right before we were about to sing, one lady in the choir room began to pray right there and then with me. She didn't pray about healing, just for comfort. I prayed for God's will, and I hoped God's will would be for Jimmy to live.

"You know, I admired Jimmy so much. During our visits to Baltimore before and after Christmas, his attitude was remarkable. He laughed a lot like he always did. Then, we would take him to radiation and I'm thinking, 'Can this really be happening?' I was in a daze. He seemed to not want anyone else to worry. His concern was for others—the girls and you. He was so willing to let you go on with your life, too.

"Then, in February, when he came here to San Antonio, he figured out the VCR, we played Scrabble and I remember making him chipped beef on toast. He always loved chipped beef on toast. I've often thought that we should have talked more, that the visit wasn't in-depth enough, that it was my fault. I have thought that maybe we ought to have talked more seriously. I know I wanted to be with him every minute he was here. We did talk about things that had happened in the past. I wish we'd talked more about our lives together and what we meant to one another. There were things I wish I had told him. If I had the opportunity now, I'd tell him how really special he was. It's funny how you tell other people these things, but you don't tell the person.

"Jimmy never had the least bit of ego, but he had a lot of intelligence and talent that I really appreciated, and I don't know if I ever told him that enough. It was hard to put him on the plane back to Baltimore, except for the fact that I was so grateful he had come.

"He slipped a lot after that and I really realized it in California—that he was dying. We were just glad to be with him at that time, knowing he would be celebrating no more birthdays. Even when we were there, though, I put the dying out of my mind so that I could enjoy the moment.

"It's amazing, but I slept so well every night we were with you all in California. I think, 'How could I when Jimmy's in his last hours?' I think God just gave me peace. After we got there, when I was alone with him, I talked to him about God. In our church, it's really important. I asked him: 'Do you believe in Jesus, that he's God's son and that he died for us?' He said, 'Yes, I do.' I said, 'That's all I need to know.' Ellen, I want to see him again.

"On his birthdays, I listen to the tape he made. I don't think Jim ever has. The sound of his voice—it brings him back for a little while. I think it's really neat that we still have his voice.

"Jimmy was a wonderful person, and it was his time to go. I've been able to accept it because of my faith. I have been able to comfort a lot of people because of it. I had never been with anybody when they died. There is something about being with a person when it's the last breath they take. There was a sadness, but there was a peace, too. I miss him, sometimes terribly, but I don't have any anger. I probably should have. The only time I really get angry is when somebody does my husband wrong. At least Jimmy had all those years. They were wonderful years."

JIM

"A constant aching, a lasting grief"—that's how Jim describes the loss of his oldest child and namesake.

When he learned of the diagnosis, he said "my initial thought was that it would be pretty tough and that there would be a long recovery. I also thought that if anybody could make it, Jimmy could. If there was one person who could survive this he would be the one," Jim told me as we talked on a bench at a theme park in San Antonio.

"I wasn't frightened. I had a pretty strong belief and faith in his strength, our strength, and a faith in the people around him. I really thought the Lord would watch out for him, whatever was possible. I never got angry at the Lord, at people, at the illness. As I understand anger, I wasn't angry.

"Right up until the time we got the call that he had only a few days left, I still had a positive attitude that he could beat the thing. He was intelligent. He was vocal. He never lost, as far as I could see, the will to defeat it, to overcome it. Even in those very last minutes, as I was rubbing his legs, his strength gave me strength. He projected that strength and attitude to others. You did the same. We all knew the odds, yet I never questioned his strength. When we got the call, all I could think of was: 'I've got to get there and be supportive. That strength Jimmy has—I've got to absorb it.' I knew he was suffering and I knew the odds were against us, but I didn't lose faith. For the twenty-four hours after that call, I thought a lot about it, relived the past, thought about what the future might hold. He was my namesake, the one who carried my name. The name is gone. Still, I thought that maybe even though the nurse told you he was dying, that maybe she was wrong. I never lost hope till I got to your house. At previous times, he had always had a glimmer. This time, the glimmer was gone.

"It was bad. I recognized then he was dying, that he'd never get better. His strength was gone, but his courage was still there. I could read it in his eyes. I wanted him to know I was there. I talked to him about his younger days. I'd ask him: 'Do you remember when we went to ballgames? Do you remember when you broke your arm playing football? One time, you missed a tackle but another time you caught a pass.' I remembered when he came home from college and wanted a Gant shirt. He was goofy over those shirts. I gave him the money for them. He never really responded to what I was saying, but he'd shake his head and sometimes I'd see a smile on his mouth.

"I told him not to fear death—that he'd led a good life, that he'd made a contribution. He was fighting death. You know him. I told him, 'Don't fight it, Jimmy. Just relax.' He was struggling, struggling, and finally, he just kind of floated away. I felt it rubbing his knees. They were cold. I knew his circulation had just about stopped. I really believe my faith never left me—or his strength. He died with strength. He taught me a lot by his manner, how he treated other people.

"One of the most difficult things in my life was watching that man take Jimmy away. I don't like to talk about it. I shouldn't have let him touch Jimmy. I should have said, 'This is no way. You can't do this. Stop. This is a man. This is my son.' It reminds me of other times in my life when I haven't been assertive enough. I think about that day whenever I fail to kick butt about something. It won't leave me. I really don't want it too, either.

"I think about Jimmy now mostly when he was a kid, a younger man. We had a good relationship, but it was different with the two older children, and the two younger children. It was almost as if we had two families. When Jimmy was a boy, I was wrapped up in work. Family was important, but work was important, too. I always talked about my kids, but at that stage in life I was focused on my job. I gave my job more time in the early years. I thought that was what I was supposed to do.

"I have a sentimental desire for Jimmy to still be around. He was my first child, my namesake, the father of my grandchildren. But in the last twenty years, we weren't around him every day. I felt almost a stronger grief when we moved to Israel and Jimmy stayed behind in the U.S. for college. That made me ache. He was the first one to leave, and this was the first time we'd ever gone off without him.

"I am sure Jimmy was tuned in to the odds all the time, but he never let any of us know. He did not permit it to come through, even on that last tape he made. I tell a lot of people about the tape. On purpose, I haven't listened to it in the last year or so. I pick it up and look at it and touch it. It's not that I'm afraid to listen to it. It's something I've heard and fully understand. I can almost recite it word for word. Maybe I would hurt, and that's why I don't listen to it. I'm getting older now, I'm in my seventies, and those realities Jimmy discussed are becoming more apparent to me. But I like his voice. I play his music, all those folk songs he did, so that I can hear his voice, and be close to him again."

CHAPTER
6

A GOOD GRIEF

I have never felt more alive than during the months Jim was dying. Home was a precipice, a place where the air was thin, but the view revealed truths I had never before known. At times, I felt drenched with insight.

There was a fullness to the days, a sharpness of focus. In that climate, I discovered my bare self. Where some might have seen only bruises, I felt a ripening.

Even when most afraid, I could wrap my arm around Jim and find relief in the simple act of touching his face or rubbing his hand. When I sighed, he was there, taking my broken pieces and cradling them in his heart. Our lives were propelled not by promise, but by rich moments that offered everything from giddiness to grace.

When Jim died, a silence began living in the house. Sometimes, I'd go half a day or more and suddenly realize I had not uttered a word. My cheerleading days were over. I had lost my voice.

An emotional exile, I traveled low to the ground in space that seemed temporary, borrowed. The days I inhabited now were unstable and long; I didn't trust my footing. As soon as I woke up in the morning, I would look at the wind-up clock on the old oak school desk beside the bed and count the hours until I could sleep again. I became an intimate of the darkness, which cloaked me in its black veil.

My hunger for Jim fed me, and I looked for him

everywhere. One afternoon walking down 24th Street in San Francisco, I heard a motorcycle cough behind me. I couldn't see the biker's face, but wisps of brown hair curled out from under the back of his helmet, and his legs, lean and taut, reminded me of Jim's. I began to follow him.

Twenty-fourth Street, where it cuts through my old neighborhood, hosts an eclectic mix of restaurants, shops and apartments. It's a lazy street where no one drives fast. Picking up my pace, I hurried down the sidewalk in the motorcycle's wake. Just as the distance widened between us, and I feared he was lost to me, the biker paused for a stop sign, allowing me to catch up. After three blocks, he parked the bike in front of a health-food store, swung one leg in a perfect arc over the leather seat, and stood. As he reached up to remove his helmet, I turned away.

One thing about grief—it doesn't let you in on its travel plans. In the middle of a conversation with a blue-suited executive or standing in a grocery line next to a woman chatting on about the price of avocados, I would remember Jim was dead and that I would never see him again. I struggled to trap the bad news inside me. This was knowledge that had to be accepted slowly, carefully, one piece at a time.

You never know what will trigger the sadness—walking through the men's section in a department store; seeing a woman lean into her boyfriend while they wait at a corner for the light to change; anniversary cards in a stationery store; a lyric from a familiar song floating out of a passing car.

Nor is it possible to predict what will trigger the anger. Shortly after Jim died, I was standing outside a store looking blankly into space when a man turned to me and said: "You look like you've just lost your best friend. Where's your smile?" For months, I received as personal assaults such casual remarks as "I could have died" and "I feel dead" and "She looked like death warmed over." One morning, I nearly ran down a group of teenage skateboarders. "You idiots," I yelled, jumping out of my car. "I could have killed you!" In those dark days, I was afraid everyone was going to die.

Then there are the well-meaning questions people ask: Are you married? What does your husband do? Dead? How? Cancer, did he smoke?

The world outside the apartment had become a dangerous, demanding place. Questions usually require answers; far too many of these begged the past tense. For me, the only safe place was home.

     *   *   *   *   *   *   *   *

For many months, the apartment on Grandview was my ground conductor, the one place I felt connected, the only place that gave me shape. In the pink of the evening, I'd sit in the recliner Jim had insisted on buying before we left Baltimore, gaze out of the window and wait for the loneliness to rip through me in gushes. So pronounced was Jim's absence it seemed a presence, something just beyond human sight.

After Jim died, my periods stopped and my hair began to fall out. When I showered, hair would come out in wet handfuls and clog the drain. A doctor told me I was under stress.

I longed to talk to Jim about all this. He would have had a lot to say. Communication was his currency, and it is what I missed most. We had developed a language of which I was the sole surviving speaker. I had become the custodian of our memories. I grew terrified of forgetting something.

Working for *The Baltimore Sun* in San Francisco, I mentally operated in two time zones—mine and the newspaper's. I would wake up at 7:00, and think of it as 10:00. Ed Goodpaster, my editor, would ask for a story by 8:00, which for me meant five o'clock. After a while, the three-hour time difference fused within me and, so, for a time, it was with Jim. I tried living for both of us.

I processed my day through the filter of what Jim might think or do. How would he react? What would he advise? It could be something as simple as hearing a new song I thought he might have enjoyed, or seeing Belgian waffles on a breakfast menu and knowing that is what *he* would have ordered. Would he have liked my new perm or preferred my hair the old way? How would he suggest I handle a fight with my mother? What would he have me say when Anne announces she's dropping out of high school and Aimée reveals how much life frightens her?

For months, I felt Jim summing me up and cheering me on. It seemed he was at the edge of things—out of reach but close enough to call in case of an emergency.

Jim was one of those people you immediately felt comfortable with. If you knew him, even just a tiny bit, you wanted more. He was such an important part of my physical self, my social self and my emotional self that I let him go the only way I knew how: slowly.

In the weeks after he died, I'd crawl into bed and play the tape he had made so that I could fall asleep to the sound of his voice. After a while, it didn't matter what he said, only that he say it. His voice, purring at me from the end of the bed, tucked me in at night, lessening the loneliness that had become my center of gravity.

Everybody has a sound you can tell a person by, a sound that announces him. Jim's was the crush of leather. Often, I would hear him before I saw him. The sound of his leather jacket moving in step with his body usually gave him away. Sometimes, in the long nights after he died, I'd twirl Jim's jacket around the living room as if it were an imaginary dance partner, just to hear that sound again.

I began to read the obituaries, paying particular attention to the age of the deceased, the cause of death and whether there was a surviving spouse. I developed instant empathy with the folks who existed among the death notices, and I wondered how they were managing.

Had they discovered that it wasn't always the anguish that was so cutting, but the simple rituals of everyday life?

Vacuuming under the bed one Saturday morning, I found a list Jim had scribbled of people he had intended to write thank-you notes to: "Millie and Frank—pyjamas. Mick and Dick—housewarming plant. Martin—teddy bear." He never did get the chance to write those thank-yous. For the longest time after he died, I couldn't understand what had caused the white paint to chip so horribly at the base of the door frames in the bedroom and office, until it struck me with the force of a sucker punch that Jim himself had chipped the paint pushing through the doors in his wheelchair. Many months after his death, I was rooting mindlessly through a drawer in the bathroom when Jim's blue brush turned up, hair clinging to its black bristles as if he had just used it. I fell to my knees and began brushing my hair.

There are only two personal things of Jim's I have kept—the leather jacket and that blue brush.

*   *   *   *   *   *   *   *

That first year, Mother and Dad telephoned just about every morning between 7:30 and 8:00 because they knew it would make waking up a little less lonely.

One morning I told Mother how much I missed hearing Jim tell me I was pretty. A small, Victorian mirror arrived in the mail a few days later.

"Whenever you forget why Jim found you beautiful, look in the mirror. You will see just what he did," Mother wrote in her note. "Grief is the mirror of love. Now, you've known both. Look in the mirror and understand."

Certain truths have a way of helping you breathe. If grief was a mirror of love, then I could trust it. It would support me, no matter how hard I fell. Grief wasn't a detour; it was the path. In a poem called "The Waking," Theodore Roethke writes, "I learn by going where I have to go." That day, I started to move again.

I was afraid, too, that if I didn't tend to it then, it would come pounding on my door later, demanding my attentions like a crazed bill collector with a past-due notice. For a time, the loss crowded out everything else, driving me to a purer kind of concentration. I know that you cannot search for serenity the way you search for a lost set of keys, though at times I sadly tried. Sometimes, the best way to find something is to stop looking for it.

Grief, I discovered, cannot be hurried. Some days, I woke up so grateful to be alive, receiving the very awakening as a gift—something to be opened, examined and enjoyed. But a few hours later, tears standing in my eyes, I would pull out the mirror, lean my face against it, and watch the two circles of fog form under my nose. Then, feeling like an imposter, I'd practice smiling. Theodore Roethke also said, "This shaking keeps me steady."

* * * * * * * *

My first story after Jim died took me to Arizona. Actually, there were two stories—one on the governor's race and another on an ancient land dispute between the Navajo and Hopi tribes.

On the plane to Phoenix, the businessman beside me asked me to have dinner with him that night. He was a good-looking man with active, blue eyes built into an open, friendly face. He had made me laugh.

"I can't."

"You're married?"

"I was married."

"If you're not married, then have dinner with me."

"He just died—my husband. Less than a month ago. No, thank you."

A few minutes later, the man mumbled something and moved to another seat. When I walked past him in the airport after we landed, he looked away.

That night, eating dinner alone at a restaurant at the Biltmore, I cried over grilled swordfish while a three-piece combo washed the room in love songs, and two couples danced the tango.

Walking across the hotel grounds back to my room, a loneliness covered me like the thick desert air. Death is high-concept stuff, but in the end it boils down to this:

I missed hanging out with Jim, being part of that creation that was bigger than both of us. When the man on the plane asked if I was married, I was unsure of the reply.

This was a messy business. How long would it take until I felt good in my own skin again? How many more afternoons would I look at a clock at 4:25, and think: This is the time Jim died, he's dying now. It has been 25 days since he died—26, 27, 28. I have been alone now for 29 days—30, 31, 32.

At night, during those first weeks, I would visualize the last time Jim and I had made love. Even now, years later, it is a frozen flash of memory that is a piece of my core.

It was late November, a couple of weeks before the diagnosis, and I had returned to Baltimore that night after a week's vacation. Jim had been sick most of the week I had been gone, taking refuge in our dark bedroom, hoping to still the commotion in his head. He hardly ever napped and I teased him about pining for me.

We danced in the living room that night to old Motown songs. Later, Jim peeled off my clothes and stared at my body, as if he were memorizing me. He made love with an uncommon urgency, and held me so tightly afterward it was hard to breathe. Jim didn't often say "I love you," but that night he shouted it.

Not long after he died, I dreamt we were making love again. My hands found the curve in the small of his back and I pulled him closer to me. Our eyes locked together as we moved, and I could feel the sweat start to slicken my chest. Looking at Jim, I began to cry full-throttle sobs. That's how I woke up, crying. I was so happy to have been with him again. For those few moments, he had come back for me.

In Jim's absence, I coupled with the grief, fastening myself to the sadness with fierce attachment. The pain had carved out a home inside me, and rather than push it away, I turned toward it. It filled my hollow spaces, creating an odd fullness. Without it, I feared, I would go limp.

*   *   *   *   *   *   *   *

Before leaving Arizona, I drove to the top of a dusty tan mesa that houses an ancient Hopi village.

Imperceptible from a distance, the village overlooks the unbroken desert floor from a vantage point that is not quite sky and not quite earth. It is as close to the top of the world as I have been.

The desert can be an uncompromising and inhospitable host, but it has fed its people for centuries, nourishing their roots and traditions.

On that yellow afternoon, I was aware of only two things: the changing light of the mesa and an almost holy silence that held the roughly-cut land in a reassuring embrace, throwing a hush over human concerns. There was no calendar here, no past or future, just a single timelessness, and a tenderness, as palpable as the heat on my face.

CHAPTER
7

ECHOES

I am so accustomed to people dying from cancer that when my mother didn't die, I guess I was surprised.

The phone call came in January 1992, five years after Jim's death. "Not again, not her, not now," I thought after saying goodbye to my father, who had told me doctors had found a tumor in her esophagus.

A few weeks later, shortly after 8:00 on a Monday morning, two surgeons in green pyjamas sliced open Mother's chest, cut out her esophagus and poured five pints of blood (one of them mine) into her body.

It was January 30, and Mother had not been able to swallow comfortably since October. Even before that, in August, she had begun to clear her throat almost constantly: "A-hem, A-hem." It's not exactly a word, that raspy sound that climbed out of her mouth from somewhere south of her throat, but it had become a part of her vocabulary. Mother is a small person, only five feet, and during those months she seemed to shrink. She couldn't swallow, so she didn't eat.

Mother can recite the dates of each doctor's appointment, starting with the first one on October 21, 1991, her 57th birthday.

"Now, calm down," the internist told Mother, who felt certain she had a serious throat disease. "You've probably convinced yourself you've got cancer."

"That's exactly right," my mom said. "That's just what I feel."

The tests they gave her that afternoon didn't set off any alarms, but it's a day she revisits, angrier and angrier each time, when her head goes crazy at night.

She had seen a couple of specialists and undergone diagnostic tests over the fall, but it wasn't until mid January that doctors discovered the tumor that had moved into her esophagus. Lying under a probe on a hospital table, Mother heard the doctor say he had spotted *something*. The next thing she knew he was calling out its measurements like a quarterback announcing his next play.

"I'm so sorry to tell you this," Dr. Donald Rosenblatt told her in an office consultation afterward. "I've only just met you. You have a growth on your esophagus and it has to come out."

Mother tried to conjure up a mental diagram of an esophagus and couldn't. She heard nurses chatting in the hallway outside, and she was wondering how she was going to tell my dad.

"But do we know for sure it's malignant?" Mother asked, slipping already into the collective "We" patients tend to use with their doctors.

"All I can tell you is that it has to come out," Dr. Rosenblatt said. "I really am sorry."

Mother found the reply evasive, yet affirmative. A lot of months had gone by since the act of swallowing had required the talents of a contortionist.

"Mrs. Uzelac," she heard the doctor saying. "If you begin to cough up blood, report to the emergency room right away. Mrs. Uzelac, do you want me to have a nurse call your husband?"

Mother signaled no, and walked in a daze out to the parking lot. She and my father had been married thirty-seven years. I suppose they know one another as well as two people can.

"What do I tell him?" Mother asked herself during the six-mile drive home from Kaiser Hospital.

"How do I tell him?"

She found Dad among his cherished auto parts in their garage, where he was rebuilding a cream-colored 1953 MG.

He looked up when Mother opened the door.

"What's wrong, Mary? What did they say?"

"Milt, we've got to talk. I'm going upstairs. Come lie down beside me for a little while."

In those next hours, they cried, talked and held one another. By chance, I telephoned that evening, and when I heard my father's dead voice answer "Hello," I knew something was wrong.

I recognized the leaden voice of grief. I understood the language, and when I looked at my father's haunted face a few days later, I saw my own reflected in it.

Listening to Dad talk on the telephone that night restored the dangerous edge to my memory. There are things you think you will never forget—until you have forgotten you ever knew them. I used to believe that if I understood a truth, it would stay with me forever. Now, I know that even the most elemental truths can be elusive and that we have to work hard every day to keep them a part of us.

A month earlier I had accepted a buy-out that had been offered to employees of *The Baltimore Sun*, which, like a lot of companies, was trying to reduce costs by cutting staff. The offer was generous: a year's salary and benefits. Since Jim had died, I had wanted to write a book about grief and this seemed the time to do it. I worried about sidelining my career, and the notion of writing a book was terrifying—but even more frightening was the idea of not trying.

The night I called my folks from my rowhouse in Baltimore, I had been off work for a week and, full of myself and my plans, I had just returned from a going-away party. In a couple of days, I would be flying to northern England to visit a cousin, and after that I was bound for Lake Tahoe, the mountain community in Northern California I had selected as my writer's retreat.

"Hello," Dad had said.

With the sound of his voice, expectations and assumptions crumbled and, a few days later, instead of flying to England, I was sitting on a plane pointed toward Los Angeles.

*   *   *   *   *   *   *   *

I wasn't prepared for the sadness in the slope of Mother's shoulder as she brought the spoon of vegetable soup from the bowl to her mouth. Her face was scrunched with pain as she swallowed. She didn't know I was watching.

Seeing my mother in that unguarded moment reminded me of how much I had forgotten about Jim. I could recall events, conversations, even scenes from his illness, but they were memories that had been stripped of everything but the words to wrap them in. The fear, the tenderness, the despair, the hope—those are the things I had forgotten. In the slope of her shoulder, Mother gave them back to me.

I ran downstairs and locked myself in the bathroom, and cried tears that were a path back to Jim. I was certain Mother was dying, and I couldn't let her see my face. She told me later that a heating duct in the bathroom had carried the sound of my sobbing upstairs, broadcasting my fears in a way my face never would have.

So what would you do if you thought you were dying? If you're my mom, you clean. In the days before the surgery she tore through the house in a fury—dusting, vacuuming, rearranging closets, labeling photographs, collecting clothes for the thrift shop. She caught up on her correspondence and placed her favorite pictures of Dad and her on his side of the bed. She got her hair cut, colored and permed, bought two nightgowns for the hospital, and purchased cards for family birthdays and anniversaries that were coming up in February.

At one point she carried an armful of skirts out to the car to take to the tailor for alterations. A few hours later, I saw her rehanging them in her closet.

"Why did you change your mind?" I wanted to know.

"It occurred to me there was a chance I may not need them," Mother said, lowering her eyes.

That week, Mother dreamt she was pregnant. She said she'd felt the baby biting into her stomach with sharp, jagged teeth.

When she gave birth, the "baby" was about the age of seven, wore a helmet of "bad, blonde hair," and smelled. When she woke up, my mom rushed into the shower, turned the water as hot as she could take it and scrubbed and scrubbed the skin where just underneath a tumor was growing.

On January 27, three days before the surgery, I was sitting on a vinyl chair in a waiting room at Kaiser while

Mother was inside consulting with her surgeon, Dr. Robert Nejdl. The man seated in the apricot-colored chair next to me was tapping his foot, reading a Jehovah's Witness tract, and praying.

Across from me, Dad was reading *The Los Angeles Times*, and Barbara was talking to him. She kept flashing a button pinned to the inside of her jacket. "Expect a Miracle," it had said.

We were waiting to hear whether the cancer had spread.

"I feel like throwing up," I wrote in a notebook while the man tapped beside me. "Every time I hug Mother, there is less and less of her. Her fleshy parts are disappearing. I'm scared about what's coming. Our lives have become enlarged this past week. Everything seems exaggerated: fixing a meal, answering the phone, getting dressed in the morning. The present has asserted itself in bold-face, in capital letters. Maybe the present becomes larger than life when the future is too frightening to contemplate."

Dr. Nejdl called us into his office.

The CAT scan is clean," he told us. "There's no sign of spread."

I jumped up and down, until I felt my mother tugging at my sleeve in an attempt to contain me. Beside me, Barbie whispered, "Good. I can start feeling again."

*   *   *   *   *   *   *   *

Mother has an easy access to joy that gets its best workout when she's traveling. An aunt says she has a "motor up her butt." If she is not on a trip, she's planning her next one. When I walked into the intensive care unit after the surgery, Mother couldn't speak because her mouth had been taped shut to hold in place a blue breathing tube, and she was plugged into an array of machines that beeped and hummed. I have always thought Mother was shaped by motion. That was as still as I have ever seen her.

In those few hours, she had grown old. Her face was marbled with sweat and her skin seemed so transparent that I thought if I got close enough, I might see through it. Her body was tense, hands folded into fists. I learned over the next few weeks that her grip was a barometer of her pain. Now and then, her eyelids fluttered and a look of confusion filled up her face. Her energy was focused inward, where her body's battle was being fought.

When Mother opened her eyes, Dad bent over the metal bed and looked at her as if she was something rare. After a while, she indicated she wanted a pen and, on a piece of paper I dug out of my purse, she wrote:

"How do I call a nurse?"

"Get morphine?"

And, then:

"Paris?"

*　　*　　*　　*　　*　　*　　*　　*

Dr. Nejdl and his team had completed the operation in just under three hours, two hours short of what he had told us to expect. He had cut out the esophagus, the muscular canal that extends from just below the tongue to the stomach, and created a new one by pulling Mother's stomach up and attaching it to her throat. In essence, he had replumbed her.

He warned us that when Mother could speak, her

voice wouldn't sound the same because he had pressed "quite strenuously" the nerves around her throat. At one point, the nerves actually were "flapping in the breeze" outside her body.

Just when I thought Dr. Nejdl was ready to tie up his report with a red ribbon, he told us he had removed cancerous cells from two lymph nodes near Mother's pancreas. They had been so small they had not shown up on the CAT scan. There was no telling whether other cancer cells had entered the lymphatic system. As a preventive measure, Dr. Nejdl suggested Mother consider chemotherapy when her body was well enough to take it.

Mother was so weak and in such pain that, for the next few days, we kept the news to ourselves. I had thought of the surgery as an intellectual exercise until I saw Mother in that stale room afterward looking like the centerpiece of a science experiment. At the side of the bed, blood, urine and mucous drained into clear plastic buckets while a yellowish liquid that reminded me of egg yolk dripped from a tube in her chest. Sometimes, I just sat beside her and watched the fluids flow.

Mother looked like she had been in a streetfight—and lost. Her face was swollen, and someone had written "DON'T MOVE" across her nose on a strip of tape attached to the plastic tube that was sucking out the green gastric juices from her stomach. Her throat had been slit, and a second incision extended like a zipper from her breasts to her belly button.

Hospitals reduce patients to beggars, and for the next sixteen days my mother begged for pain relief. At first she could not shift in bed without screaming. Even before she could speak, I saw her lips moving to the Serenity Prayer, which she repeated like a mantra:

"God grant me the serenity to accept the things I cannot change; Courage to change the things I can; And wisdom to know the difference."

I noticed that Mom and Dad had begun to talk about "the surgery" instead of "the cancer," and "healing" instead of "curing." With a nailed-on smile, Mother preened for her doctors, an intimate gesture in so formal a setting, and she affected a kind of nonchalance, as if she had just popped in for the day. Yet every time a doctor left her bedside, her slate-blue eyes would follow him with a hunted look, as though the doctor himself was withholding the cure.

As a mother would an infant, I became alert to Mom's sounds and facial expressions. I fed her, turned her, bathed her, and it was on this physical plane that we existed for weeks. When Mother spoke, she talked in the low, gravelly voice sick people use. It could have been Jim speaking. Sometimes, her face filled up with a faraway, haunted look, her thoughts sealed behind glassy eyes.

Periodically, nurses came in to turn Mother over, or to weigh her, or to take a blood sample or temperature. Mom took to calling her catheter, "Cath—that little pisser," and we laughed when we learned every patient on her floor was waiting to pass gas, a measure of success that moves patients closer to the exit sign and out the front door.

During those days I massaged Mother's legs, gave her bed baths, carried her to the toilet and sprayed her hair with the same brand of dry shampoo I had used on Jim. Mother practically purred when I rubbed her scalp with her pink hairbrush. She was less pleased when I pushed her to eat. At one point, she dropped to eighty pounds.

It is odd that something so brittle as a life-threatening illness should create such tenderness among its attendants, but as my family watched over Mother, a language of cherishing returned, wrapping us in its warmth.

When I was a young girl, our family lived for three years in a small town on the shore outside Lisbon. I spoke Portuguese almost fluently, and even dreamt in it. A few years ago, I returned to Portugal for the first time since I was a teenager. I had not spoken the language in twenty years, yet the words came hurtling back, and I found myself conversing in a language I didn't even know I knew.

Looking after Mother those weeks was like returning to some distant yet familiar country, a place with its own customs, culture and language. I knew the place. I had been there with Jim.

*   *   *   *   *   *   *   *

Except for Jim, Mother has been my closest friend. Since his death, she has sheltered me with her spiritual strength and reminded me how important it is to live in the moment. That's a tough lesson. The moment I believe I have resolved my past, I begin to worry about the future: Will my mother die from this cancer? Will she leave me, my father, my sister? Have I told her everything?

Mother has night terrors about dying. My terrors come in the full light of day, filling up the empty space around me until I can no longer move. "Let go," my mother has told me through the years just when I was hanging on tightest to whatever it was I needed to release. "Let go."

During her recovery, Mother relearned how to walk, eat and speak. Even now, almost two years later, her voice sounds slightly hoarse, as if she's stretching it farther than it wants to go. It's lower, too. Once a lyric soprano, her voice currently resides a couple of notches down the scale. Mother has sung everything from opera to "Oklahoma." These days, she is lucky to make it through "Happy Birthday."

There have been other changes as well. She cannot lie flat or bend over. Fortunately, she is able to eat regular foods, but she throws up a lot. When we go to a restaurant, it no longer surprises me when she vomits into her napkin.

"Tell me what chemotherapy is like," Mother asked one afternoon when she was still in the hospital. "What was it like for Jim?"

Mother began to cry.

"Now I realize how much he suffered. I'm going to have to do the chemo, Ellen, aren't I? With the lymph nodes, we can't be sure about the future. I've always said I could die tomorrow and be happy because I've done so much in my life. But it's not OK anymore. I don't want to die tomorrow."

I closed the door of the hospital room and there was quiet, except for the sound of my mother crying. As suddenly as the tears came, they stopped.

And she started to laugh.

"Know what else? I'll be really pissed if I don't get to take my trip to Paris."

*   *   *   *   *   *   *   *

In April, three months after the surgery, Mother began preventive chemotherapy with a drug called Platinol.

"We're recommending three courses of chemotherapy,

Mrs. Uzelac," Mom's oncologist noted, swatting her prescription pad as if she were taking a dinner order.

("Ground pepper with your Platinol?")

I was reminded of Jim's medical oncologist, Dr. Minford. Whenever we saw him, he used oversized words and talked about chemical formulas while jotting things down with a black Magic Marker on a flip chart in his small, crowded office. I always expected that the next time I saw him, he'd have a plastic pen liner in his breast pocket and ink stains down his shirt.

Lying in a vinyl-covered blue recliner, Mother received her first "hit" of chemotherapy. She kept nodding off as the drug coursed its way through her body. Three times, she got up to squat on a white commode that the nurse had placed next to her chair. Chemo makes you pee a lot.

"I felt like two people today," Mother told me that night. "One part of me was unafraid, talking to other people, making light of the chemo. The other person in me was really scared. The nurse told me, too, that she's never known anyone to take this drug who hasn't lost their hair."

For the next two days, more of the chemical was flushed into Mother's body through a pump attached to her lower left arm. Every twenty hours or so, when the pump ran dry, she'd go to the hospital for a refill.

In all, she received Platinol for three consecutive days, though it works in the body for days after that, ostensibly killing lingering cancer cells. She took it three times, in April, May and June.

Mother handled the drug well, though she looked limp, as if she'd been boiled too long. Her face turned the color of the pink geraniums in her back yard, and she was hot to the touch even as she shivered under a wool blanket. She couldn't concentrate enough to read, but except for some nausea and occasional wooziness, she never got really sick. And she never had to wear the wig she'd bought. She didn't lose a hair.

"I hate going into the oncologist's office," she said after one visit. "I see all those sick people in the waiting room, and I want to separate myself from them. I wonder: Will I see them next time? Is that the way I'm going to look a few months from now?

"Under the shower the other morning, I had this desire to just clean everything away—like a paranoid. I stood under the water washing, washing and washing, and I thought maybe if I use enough soap, maybe if I get the water hot enough, I can wash it away.

"I didn't want to get out of the shower."

After her final round of chemotherapy, Mother met in the examining room with her oncologist, Dr. Joan Chlebowski.

"You've done well, very well," Dr. Chlebowski said warmly. "I wish I could give you a certificate to tell you that after three courses of chemotherapy, you've graduated."

"But I can't. No one can."

A few days later, Mother met with Dr. Nejdl, who was surprised to see her driving again. He checked her scars, and told her to take the two-month trip to Britain she and Dad had tentatively planned for the end of the summer.

"Go to Europe. Enjoy yourself," he said. "We'll see each other in a few months when you get back."

For thirty minutes, Mother waited for a man at the hospital pay phone to hang up so she could tell Dad she'd gotten the OK for their trip. The man knew she was waiting, but ignored her.

Finally, she handed him a note: "I'm pissed!"

The guy cupped the receiver in his palm, said he was pissed, too, and kept on talking.

*   *   *   *   *   *   *   *

Fourteen months after her surgery, Mother and I were sharing a hotel room on Leicester Square in London. It wasn't Paris, but it was close enough.

"I hope this doesn't surprise you or hurt you, but it wouldn't blow me away if the cancer came back again," my mother said. "I half-expect it. It would be unusual if it didn't."

It is difficult to listen to a mother talk about dying. Perhaps with a mother more than any other, there exists a promise of continuance.

But on this changing frontier, where Mother now roamed, we were members of the same tribe. "The closest bonds we will ever know are bonds of grief," Cormac McCarthy writes in the novel, "All The Pretty Horses." "The deepest community one of sorrow."

In the years since Jim had died, we had talked so much about death and hope, dreams and despair. Those talks were the pillars of our shared past, the props of our present, and they have shaped more than anything else what Mother and I are to one another.

In a sense, I have become the repository of Mother's fears.

"I try to have a positive attitude, but there's always that gnawing fear it will recur," Mother told me during our London holiday.

She didn't waste words.

"I don't even know what tense to put it in: Do I say, 'I have cancer' or 'I had cancer'? After the surgery, your father decided the cancer was gone. He deals with it the best way he knows how, and he's the one who keeps my spirits up. To him, it's history and I'm well. Well, it's not history to me. It never can be."

I learned that afternoon that my mother is afraid of the dark. All those years, I thought she had just fallen asleep with the light on.

* * * * * * * *

Mother doesn't wander through life, she collides with it, and her recovery, like everything else she does, was accompanied by a startling rush of energy. Faster than her doctors expected, she began to eat solid food, to wear a path through the length of the house, and, with Dad's arms as props, to take long, hot showers.

From the start, Dad had treated Mother's body like a machine with a malfunction. "She checked out on the blood gasses today," I'd hear him report enthusiastically into the phone after the surgery, or "We're working on getting some weight back on her." In the hospital, he had monitored constantly the dials on the pumps that were feeding her morphine, oxygen and nutrients.

"One-hundred percent oxygen, five pounds pressure," Dad would announce to no one in particular.

"Cross-check and ready for take-off," I'd reply in my deepest voice. "Take your seats please."

Some mornings, Dad and I walked through the neighborhood, and that's the only time he ever talked to me about his own fears.

"I believe it's gone. They got it all," he told me one morning. Then, a week later, "What worries me is that it will come back."

The day Mother made an appointment for her first round of chemotherapy, she hung up the phone and couldn't stop crying. Dad held her to him, patting her head. "You can't live every day under a cloud, Mary, expecting it to rain."

After Mother first came home, a visiting nurse checked in on her for a couple of weeks, then dropped us from her roster after deciding we were capable of cleaning Mother's "wounds" and changing her bandages ourselves. At the start, Mother's new plumbing created a lot of choking, vomiting and diarrhea. I knew Mom was feeling better when she began dipping into her trashy novels again. She'd fall asleep with a paperback propped on her chest and her pink dime-store glasses wrapped half-way down her face, an occurrence in our house you can set clocks by.

Mother and Dad slept those first couple of months in the guest room, the same room Jim and I had shared five years earlier during our move to San Francisco. The folks called it their cocoon, and from their bed Mother could watch the water slosh in the pool and listen to the wind whip Jim's chimes. Mornings, she'd command me to "open the window!" to get rid of the stale, sickroom smell.

Dad rarely left Mother's side during those weeks, and his fingers were nearly always wrapped in hers. "I love you, Mary," he'd say, over and over. The way he uttered them, there was magic in the words. They never talked about the cancer, only "getting stronger."

Gradually, tentatively, Mother and Dad began to talk about the future—a trip, perhaps, to Lake Tahoe or Hawaii in the spring, musings about where we'd be on my next birthday. I had celebrated my 36th that year in "the cocoon."

There is something strangely healing about that room, whose low, king-size bed was easier for Mom to get in and out of than her own. Tending to Mother in the same room that had been Jim's refuge when he was so sick pushed me outside of time's limits. I'd look at Mother and see Jim's face. When she spoke, it was his voice I heard.

I had left my job to write about a husband's cancer, not to take care of a mother's. Yet, helping care for her lighted the dark corners of my memory. For many days, my hand raced across my notebook, retrieving what I'd lost. To some extent, Mother gave me my voice. Until then, I had been feeling my way. Now, I was following solid tracks.

I have read somewhere that real events don't end, only stories about them do.

A few days before I left Los Angeles, we returned to the hospital to see Dr. Nejdl. It was exhausting for Mother, and when she saw the doctor she reached out to him with one hand, while throwing up in the other. In the examining room, Dr. Nejdl surveyed his handiwork, mentioning offhandedly that the numbness in Mother's jaw and neck would disappear in about six months.

"Six months, so definite a term," I thought to myself. "The time it took Jim to die in. He expects her to be alive in six months." It wasn't until that moment that I dared put Mother back into the future.

Two weeks after my mother came home, I packed up the car for the drive to Lake Tahoe, five-hundred miles to the north in the Sierra Nevada. As a parting gift, I had given my parents a copy of Dr. Seuss's "Oh, the Places You'll Go!"

My throat tightened and refused to let me speak, so

Mother read the book aloud to Dad and me. She had to stop a few times to collect her breath, and when she finished she cried as hard as I've heard a person cry.

> *"All alone!*
> *Whether you like it or not,*
> *Alone will be something*
> *you'll be quite a lot*
> *And when you're alone, there's a very good chance*
> *you'll meet things that scare you right out of your pants.*
> *There are some, down the road between hither and yon,*
> *that can scare you so much you won't want to go on.*
> *But on you will go...*
> *On and on you will hike.*
> *And I know you'll hike far*
> *and face up to your problems*
> *whatever they are."*

Looking at my folks' faces through the window as I pulled out of the driveway, I recognized the farthest reaches of myself.

I had come for a few days, and stayed for five weeks, a stop in a journey that continues still.

"Your mountain is waiting," Mother had just read to me. *"So get on your way!"*

I drove north on Route 99, one of those has-been roads whose scenery is patched together with rust heaps, run-down motels and abandoned fruit stands. Flowering peach and almond trees filled the car with a sweetness, and from time to time I'd see a lone farmer walking his fields, fingering the rich, spring soil.

CHAPTER
8

FINDING AND KEEPING

Solitude has led me closer to my own nature, and time and again, it has brought me back to the land. I have gone to the woods, empty and bereft, and I have returned with my shape restored. It is the balm I seek when I am sure the loneliness will kill me. It is where I go when I have lost my way.

In the months after Jim died, I did not sit still long enough for a shadow to stick. Life was a series of newspaper datelines: Denver, Portland, Seattle, Los Angeles, Phoenix, Albuquerque, Reno, Salt Lake City, and all the little places in between. In every town, I was a stranger—rootless, a temporary lodger. For a time, the traveling gave me amnesia.

But grieving, like writing, is something we must do for ourselves. Now, I believe, it is the road that healed me. On its path, I carved out a home.

Even though the towns changed, I found community everywhere as I soaked up the kindnesses of strangers, recognizing in their hooded eyes losses much like my own. For a long while, I felt like a magnet for people in pain.

Along the way, I came to know the land and, like the earth around a root, it has stilled me: the blue mountains of northern New Mexico; the lush, green carpet of Oregon's Willamette Valley, the stark beauty of the Nevada desert; even—and perhaps most especially—the down-home towns decorated with tacky lawn ornaments, American flags, picket fences and satellite dishes.

At times, it has seemed as if I were driving through a painting. Once, in New Mexico, I rounded a corner in a broad valley and the mountains, rising blue and red in the distance, so startled me I had to pull over. I bent my head over the steering wheel and wept for reasons I didn't understand.

For years I thought that if I let the grief seep through me, it would one day depart, bringing a thaw after the freeze. Meanwhile, I would scour my interior, excavating the sadnesses, a piece at a time. It hasn't quite worked out that way.

There have been times I was so lonesome for another's touch that I'd rush off for a massage, just to feel hands on my body. One day my mother traveled five-hundred miles to hug me. At times I have tried to block the grief, but I know now it has staying power. Once, I smelled cigarette on a friend who had promised he had quit smoking. His kiss gave him away. That night, I dreamt his body had shriveled like Jim's, and for days after, I worried that he, too, was going to die.

At times I know I have spoken of "my husband" and "my grief" as if they were interchangeable nouns. Just recently someone asked if Jim had died of "natural causes." I wasn't sure how to respond. To me, there is nothing "natural" about the disappearance of a forty-one-year-old man. Although the years have weakened grief's hold, I suspect it will always be a presence.

Three years after Jim died, after moving back to Baltimore, I walked into the main public library to renew my membership card.

"You have late charges," the dour clerk snapped as

she scowled at her computer screen.

"What do you mean? I haven't lived in Baltimore in almost four years."

She turned the screen toward me.

Three books—all borrowed by Jim before we had moved to the West Coast—had been returned after the due date. The fine: $4.28.

I left my money on the counter, walked to the sidewalk and took a deep breath.

There is no statute of limitations on grief.

Still, I cannot say I regret the way the grief continues to insinuate itself into my life. It reminds me I am human. It humbles me.

It has enlarged my sympathies and opened the world up to wider interpretation, creating a wholeness larger than before. There is no old *self* to reclaim.

On the fourth anniversary of Jim's death, my aunt Dorothy, widowed herself at the age of forty-eight, gave me a book of quotations. She had placed a book marker beside this quote attributed to Mark Twain: "Grief can take care of itself, but to get the full value of a joy, you must have somebody to divide it with."

* * * * * * * *

When I think of pivotal moments, my mind wanders back to Peter, whom I knew for a few months, and to Ruth, whom I knew for only a few hours.

Peter brought back the joy, and Ruth showed me how to speak.

Five months after Jim died, I went out on my first date. Peter and I looked so much alike we could have passed for brother and sister. Our skin tone was an almost exact match. Our hair, too. He was a saxophone player who had suffered wrenching losses of his own, I learned later. I'll never forget his eyes—the color of overcast skies—or the way a song could transform his face.

"Don't you think it's too soon?"

I was excited about having met Peter, and had called one of my oldest friends to tell her about him. It didn't occur to me to curb my enthusiasm.

"It hasn't been a year since Jim died," my friend said. "I couldn't do it. It's not right. It's too soon."

Divorcees go dancing, I'm told. Widows stay home.

Loneliness isn't some sort of abstraction. It's a raw ache, a restlessness with no shut-off valve. For months I had set the dinner table for one. I hadn't bothered to play the stereo because the silence was so loud, and at night, when I crawled between the sheets, I willed the telephone to ring. After a while, you run out of friends to call.

During the dying and just after, I had felt singled out and special, loaded with purpose. There had been an almost theatrical quality to life. Then, it seemed, I turned into a cardboard character in a flat world.

Peter lifted me outside myself, reminding me I was alive, restoring spontaneity to my days. I hadn't been sure I would ever again get giddy over a phone call, or rush to the mail box at the end of a day, or find comfort in the curve of a lover's arms. Just the knowledge that such things were possible gave me hope. With Peter, I climbed out of a tomb.

Some bereavement therapists say it takes three years to resolve a death-loss. Four years if it's a child or a young spouse. If there is one thing I know it is this: You cannot reduce grief to a mathematical formula.

It takes as long as it takes.

Not long after I met Peter, I lifted the gold wedding band from my fourth finger and examined the pale circle of skin beneath it. A buttery crescent moon hanging among the stars over San Francisco pulled my eyes skyward. It wasn't the darkness that had drawn my attention. It was the light.

The next day I took our two wedding rings to a jeweler with a rough sketch of what I had seen in the night sky. The jeweler melted the gold together and created a pendant of a crescent moon. A small diamond sits in the moon's curve.

Ever since, I have worn the crescent moon around my neck.

* * * * * * * *

When I first met Ruth she was sitting on her son's piano bench, which had been polished to a high chestnut gloss. She was wearing pearls and a blue satin dress.

Ruth's son had died of AIDS two weeks before Jim. They would have been the same age, and we lived in the same neighborhood. I was researching a story about parents, mothers mostly, who come to San Francisco to accompany their sons through their dying. They come to help their grown sons cut up their food, to select music for a memorial service, to keep the nightmares at bay.

When Ruth's son John died, his body was reduced to a shell, his voice incapable of a whisper. He could not walk. He could not speak. He could not eat. And, finally, he stopped breathing.

"Family and friends are around you, just as you wanted," the home nurse wrote in her medical log that day. "The room was filled with love. Goodbye, John."

As I listened to Ruth talk, I recognized my own voice, but I was too frightened to claim it. I didn't tell her Jim had died two weeks after John. Or that they would have been the same age. Or that I was hurting, too. After all, she was there to disclose. I was just taking notes. This wasn't about me.

After an hour I got up to leave and as I shook her hand goodbye, I started to cry.

"I should have told you in the beginning, my husband died four months ago, same as John, in May. I hurt for you Ruth, I really do."

Ruth took my hand, and led me back to the couch. "You do understand, don't you?"

For just a moment, we held one another, then Ruth began to talk about truths.

"It's very difficult. You want to hold onto him no matter what. You want just one more day—to think you can look at his face for just one more day," she said. "I sometimes felt like we were on a journey, John and I, and I was privileged to go along part of the way with him. Even though I knew he would leave me here, I was glad I was able to go with him part of the way."

Grief has its own language. Ruth wasn't just telling me her story. She was handing me her heart. I only saw her that one time, but with Ruth, I came out of hiding.

*   *   *   *   *   *   *   *

Jim used to say that people never remembered him. "I've gone through most of my life with a complex about being remembered," he wrote in a letter to me a few months before he became ill. "I can recall so many instances when I was forgotten or overlooked or not

133

noticed at all. I expect people to get my name wrong, I
expect them not to recall my face and I am ready for
them to think my contributions actually came from
someone else."

As he got older, however, he began to enjoy "being
in the background, behind the scenes" and he would
marvel when "somebody actually remembers me."

For so long, Jim occupied the grooves in the floors I
paced, the corners of every room I entered, the space
between each blade of grass in my yard. Now, in the
quiet distance between us, I revisit him in memories
that no longer torment, but soothe.

Not remember?

I remember the way he put on his shoes, how he
brushed his teeth in the shower, how he twisted his hair
between his fingers when he talked. In re-imagining our
lives together, I have sniffed for clues, searching for some
sort of understanding.

"Memory is more than a looking back to a time that
is no longer," Frederick Buechner writes in his memoir,
"The Sacred Journey." "It is a looking out into another
kind of time altogether where everything that ever was
continues not just to be, but to grow and change with
the life that is in it still. The people we loved. The people
who loved us. The people who, for good or ill, taught us
things. Dead and gone though they may be, as we come
to understand them in new ways, it is as though they
come to understand us—and through them we come to
understand ourselves—in new ways too."

* * * * * * * *

After unearthing my memories and exploring my

interior, I have begun to appreciate what rests outside my own front door: A purple larkspur bloomed yesterday, and this morning a delicate orange champagne bubble popped up beside it. I have watched the blue mountain jays peck at my petunias, and I have listened to them screech as they chase one another through the tall pines around my log cabin. Just one-quarter mile from my house there is a lake that calls out to me. It knows my name.

Most mornings I walk four miles along a bike path bordered now with wildflowers. I sing while I walk. For four months last winter the path was covered with mountains of snow, so each summer day seems like a gift. I almost ache when I think about summer ending, but I can already smell it in the air.

I moved to Lake Tahoe to write about loss, but what I've found is a wholeness and a home that resides within me. If "home" is a feeling of being anchored, I have found it in the late afternoon sunlight that turns the green needles of the pines a shimmery silver; in the meteor showers that sprayed the black sky with white light a few nights ago; in the roar of a gushing waterfall near my favorite reading spot.

I don't know how much longer I'll be here, but the mountains have disclosed truths I hope always to carry in my heart. Once, while sitting alone at the lake, I actually felt a warmth, as if someone were holding me. For the first time in a long while I felt safe, and it is that feeling that has diminished my loneliness and filled me with awe and unspeakable hope.

Next week Aimée will visit, and Anne called just now, "to check in," as she put it. Each of us is back in California, living only three hours apart. I think of our migration here as another of Jim's legacies. It was loss that brought Aimée and Anne and me together—but it was through that loss that we found and kept one another. They are part of my shading, part of my texture, and on some level I know I am part of theirs. In the end, the best thing we can do for ourselves is to be there for one another.

I realized the other day that I don't own a calendar, and it has skewed my sense of time. I have no sense of days stacked one after the other, grouped by month and year, by week and weekend. For me, every day is an equal. Yet, I hear the clock ticking—and I know it is marking time for me.

Even though the hurting has stopped, the grief pushes me still to explore *this* day, *this* moment. It has taught me that this moment is all I am certain of having.

Life is not a continuum, but a series of journeys. I often have felt I have lived many lives in this short one. For me, the journey is more important than the destination. It is that series of key moments that make up a life. I hope never to stop moving.

EPILOGUE

People frequently ask whether writing about Jim's death and its aftermath has furthered my own grief. For months I shrugged off the question. I figured I couldn't have done the writing unless I was pretty well settled in my "Self."

That much is true, I realize now, but there's more. I needed to write this book in the same way a tree sheds its leaves, or a salmon swims upstream. There was an inevitability to it.

For me, *Lost & Found* is part-monument, part-offering, part-affirmation. Long before I fastened onto the notion of writing a book, I began tracking my grief in a journal. As memories or feelings or thoughts unfolded, I would record them. Shreds of sentences, ideas, phrases — they are all here in a sack beside my chair, grief's trail scratched out on paper napkins, sales receipts, ticket stubs, matchbooks. I think of these curious bits of paper as mile markers in my journey.

The most wonderful thing about writing *Lost & Found* was also the most difficult: revisiting the past. There were times I collapsed onto the couch, leveled by memories too painful to be in the same room with. For days at a time I wouldn't even turn on the computer. But memory manages to throw out as much joy as pain, and I have laughed as hard as I have cried. Often, too, during the writing, I have recalled Jim's strength, and I have leaned into it when I felt my own resolve weaken.

I have discovered an eerie parallel between writing

and grieving. Each is a lonely, private exercise, but reward comes inevitably in those exhilarating moments that offer transcendence, a vista into the heart.

Neither writing nor grief can ever be fully completed. I could tinker with the words in this book until I have no words left. As with grief, there comes a time when we must let go.

On the sixth anniversary of Jim's death, which passed a few months ago, I took roses to the lake, one for each year he's been gone. It is a ritual I observe every year. Only this time, as I tossed out the roses, they kept returning to me, borne back by the current. And, so it is with grief.

A few years ago, when I thought new memories about Jim could no longer be made, I walked into my parents' back yard and marveled at the size of the lemons on my dad's tree.

"What have you been doing to the tree, Dad? The lemons are huge."

My father gave me an odd glance, and then turned toward my mother.

"Should I tell her, Mary?"

"Tell me what?"

My father took my hand, and led me over to the tree.

"The day we came home from spreading Jim's ashes, I looked into the box and realized it wasn't empty. I wasn't sure what to do, so I spread the rest of Jim's ashes here, at the base of the lemon tree. I'd remembered how much he liked the tree when you visited that March. Ever since, its fruit has been bountiful. I can't come out here and not think of him."

When my father told me that story, three years had passed since Jim's death.

A few days ago, I found a poem by Goethe that I shared with my dad:

"Know you the land where lemon-trees bloom? ...A soft wind hovers from the sky, the myrtle is still and the laurel stand tall—do you know it well?

There, there, I would go, O my beloved, with thee!"

* * * * * * * *

Mother once told me she hopes there are different regions of Heaven so that when she dies she might hop a cloud and travel. "Can you imagine?" she said, elated at the prospect. "An East Heaven, a North Heaven!" Mother is loopy about travel and so am I. As I write this, we're both planning journeys.

Mother and Dad will leave in a few days for seven weeks in France. "For some reason, the number bothers people," my father told me the other day. "It's not even enough. Why not four weeks, folks want to know, or six weeks?" My parents have selected their favorite paintings by the French impressionists and they are going to search out the coastlines, the gardens, and the urban landscapes that inspired them. Mother, finally, is going to Paris. I have never seen her more excited about a trip.

Tomorrow I leave for Montana. I am going because it is a place I've never been. The trees have already begun to turn color there, and last week the first snow fell. If I breathe deeply enough, I imagine I can already smell wood smoke in the air and the crisp scent of autumn.

A friend who travels often wrote recently, "To my mind, one of the greatest gifts of travel is the gift of vulnerability. On the road, you just have to become vulnerable. You can't get around it, so you might as well accept it and say, "OK, world, I'm at your disposal. Take good care of me, please."

Traveling challenges us, increases us and eventually brings us home.

Lake Tahoe, California
September 24, 1993

ACKNOWLEDGMENTS

When I say I could not have written this
book without the encouragement of my parents,
it is one of the truest things I know. From the
beginning, their support has been unswerving.
They are my fiercest fans, and my best friends.

———————

Heartfelt thanks go to my sister, Barbara,
who was there for Jim and me during the toughest
times, and gave of herself again during the writing
of the book. Barbie, I am grateful—for then
and for now.

———————

Terry Jones, a Baltimore Sun editor,
has ventured down grief's path with me twice.
He was a steady friend after Jim died, and, as an
editor, he has generously pored over these pages,
adding his own talents to Lost & Found.

———————

My appreciation also goes to my agent,
Jessica Wainwright, of The Literary Group. Finally,
I cannot wrap up this project without thanking
Ed Goodpaster, who, in his own crazy way,
has helped me keep sane.

BIOGRAPHY

*Ellen Uzelac, a former national correspondent
and West Coast Bureau Chief for The Baltimore Sun,
files freelance stories for national magazines
and newspapers from her home in
South Lake Tahoe, California.*

A MESSAGE FROM THE PUBLISHER

"From the first page I read of Ellen Uzelac's book proposal, I thought it would be an exceptionally well-written manuscript. By the time Ellen finished her book, I knew we had a wonderfully written story to publish. 'Lost & Found' is not a how-to manual or an academic exploration; it's Ellen's story and one we all must ultimately claim as our own."

W. R. Spence, M.D.
Publisher

Our focus at WRS Publishing is on books that inspire and educate: books about contemporary heroes who have fulfilled impossible dreams; books about survivors who have broken the bonds of grief and pain; and books from which we may learn from others who have forged their way through life experiences that are common to us all. Americans are yearning for leadership; we have complained about the negativism of our media for too long. Let our books turn your attention to present-day role models, persons who can enlighten and inspire us through the celebration of human achievement.

Call us at 1-800-299-3366 for suggestions or for a free book catalog.

WATCH FOR THESE RELATED TITLES:

AWAKE AGAIN tells the comeback story of Martin Krieg, pronounced clinically dead and paralyzed by a head injury, only to rehabilitate with a bicycle then ride across America.

FOR THE LOVE OF MIKE is the story of a family overcoming the isolation and fears when their twelve-year-old son is diagnosed with cancer.

THE GHETTO SOLUTION details how Roland Gilbert, creator of the Simba Program for African-American boys, is combatting the downward spiral that entraps inhabitants of the ghetto.

WRS
PUBLISHING
A Division of WRS Group, Inc.
Waco, Texas